Comfortable
under
Pressure

Meredith Laurence

Photography by Jessica Walker

Walah!, LLC Publishers
Philadelphia

First Edition

Published in the United States by Walah!, LLC/Publishers

walah@me.com

ISBN-10: 0-9827540-1-9
ISBN-13: 978-0-9827540-1-6

Printed in U.S.A.

Book design by Janis Boehm
www.bound-determined.com

Photography by Jessica Walker
www.jessicawalkerphotography.com

Food styling by Bonne Di Tomo, Lisa Ventura and Lynn Willis

Acknowledgements

My undying gratitude goes to Annie for doing so much to make this book happen. You tested, tasted, edited, inspired and supported me throughout - even when I was not a perfect reflection of the book's title! I'm glad you were won over by pressure-cooking (and no-one writes a better index)!

I would also like to thank the following people without whom this book would not be in your hands: Eric Theiss, Janis Boehm, Lisa Ventura, Bonne Di Tomo, Lynn Willis, Jessica Walker, Grace Lee, Joseph McAllister, Tanya van Biesen, and all the friends and neighbors who ate all the food we made.

Table of Contents

Table of Contents

Pork and Lamb

Seafood

Rice, Beans and Grains

Vegetables

Pasta and Sauces

Desserts

Introduction

My first memory of a pressure cooker was as a young child in my mother's kitchen. A brushed steel pot sat on the stove with a knob on top shaking around madly. There was a lot of hissing coming from the pot and my mother said "DON'T TOUCH THAT!" I think I share that memory with many of my generation. Consequently, for many of us, pressure cookers became scary objects – objects not to be touched. To be honest, after that incident I didn't touch one for about twenty-five years!

Since those days, however, pressure cookers have changed. You can still buy stovetop pressure cookers, but they have more safety valves built into their lids now to prevent them from exploding and making it easier to manage the pressure inside. Even easier to operate are the new electric pressure cookers. With an electric pressure cooker, all you have to do is set the time and pressure and the cooker will regulate the heat, turning off after the programmed number of minutes. That makes pressure-cooking even easier than cooking on the stovetop in a regular pot or pan.

It is the ease of pressure-cooking that led me to write a cookbook for the pressure cooker. As the Blue Jean Chef, my goal is to make people feel as comfortable in the kitchen as they are in their blue jeans, and what could make a cook more comfortable than simply setting a timer? Still, many home cooks continue to be intimidated by pressure cooking. I decided that with the right book, filled with delicious recipes, tips and information about pressure-cooking, people could become comfortable with the pressure cooker again, and feel rewarded with not only tasty meals, but with extra time on their hands. This is that book, intended to make you Comfortable Under Pressure.

About this Book

The recipes in this book were written and tested using a 6½-quart electric pressure cooker. You can certainly use other types and sizes of pressure cookers for these recipes, but I recommend nothing smaller than a 5-quart cooker, unless you convert the recipes for smaller quantities. (See **Converting Recipes** on page 15)

    I've tried to give you as much quick information as possible about each recipe, making it easier to decide what to cook. You will find this information across the top of each recipe page.

Serves	Prep	Cooking Time	Release Method
6	**Easiest**	**HIGH 10 Minutes**	**Quick**

The first piece of information is the serving size for the recipe. Most of the recipes are written for at least 6 people. After all, if you're cooking in a pressure cooker, you are probably interested in saving time, and if you're only cooking for 2 or 4, having 2 or 4 extra portions in the freezer for another occasion is a huge time saver.

    The next morsel of information is the relative ease of preparing the recipe. Many books tell you how long the prep will take. In my opinion, this is a very subjective measure – the time it takes *me* to prep a recipe may not be the same time it takes *you* to prep a recipe. So, instead of giving a number of minutes, I have created a measure of *"Easy", "Easier",* or *"Easiest"* to let you know how the recipe measures up against the other recipes in the book. In creating this scale, I took into consideration how much chopping was required, whether the food needed to be browned at the start of the recipe and roughly how long I felt those tasks would take. If you're looking for a recipe that will get into the pressure cooker the fastest, giving you time to do other things, pick an *"Easiest"* prep recipe.

    Next to the prep information is the cooking time. Just because a recipe might have the easiest prep, doesn't necessarily mean that the cooking time is just as fast. So, I've listed the cooking time at the top of the recipe so that you can quickly see what is involved. The cooking time does *not* include the time it takes the cooker to come up to pressure, which will depend on how much liquid is in the pot and how full the cooker is. It can range from 5 to 15 minutes for a pressure cooker to come up to pressure.

The last piece of information along the top bar is the release method. (See **Releasing Pressure** on page 16.) During the months it took to test all these recipes, some of my testers commented that they would have to re-read the recipe to see how to release the pressure from the cooker - a natural release or a quick-release. I thought it would be helpful to have this information clearly visible so that you don't make a mistake and quick-release the pressure when you should have done otherwise.

Finally, I wanted you to be able to quickly figure out which recipes will get dinner on the table soonest. To do this, I had to take into consideration the prep time, the cooking time **and** the release method. So, I've given each recipe a ranking of *"Quick"*, *"Quicker"* or *"Quickest"*. These ratings are again subjective, and depend on your personal skill level, but they are rated against the other recipes in this book so you'll know which recipes are the quickest for *you* to make. Whether a recipe is *"Quick"*, *"Quicker"* or *"Quickest"* is marked in the side tab of the recipe page with corresponding lightning bolts, three lightening bolts being the quickest recipes overall. Remember, all pressure cooker recipes are faster than cooking them in the traditional manner, so you're already ahead of the game!

About Pressure Cooking

A pressure cooker is a cooking vessel with a lid that locks on and prevents steam from escaping. As a result, the steam builds up pressure in the pressure cooker – about 15 pounds per square inch of pressure (15 psi) – and the temperature inside the cooker increases. At sea level, water boils at 212º F before it is converted into steam, and it cannot get any hotter than that, regardless of the heat source below it. In a pressure cooker, with 15 psi of pressure added, water boils at 250º F before being converted into steam. That means that foods inside a pressure cooker are able to cook at higher temperatures, and therefore are finished sooner – in about one third of the time it would take to cook on a regular stovetop.

The time saved in pressure-cooking is obviously a huge benefit, but there are secondary benefits to pressure-cooking as well.

Health Benefits

The main cooking medium in pressure-cooking is liquid rather than fat. When pressure-cooking, you can choose to almost eliminate fats, creating lean meals. Vegetables can be steamed quickly, retaining their crunch and color. All foods cook quickly in a pressure cooker, and foods that are cooked quickly retain more of their nutrients, minerals and vitamins.

Flavor Benefits

In a pressure cooker, the lid is sealed onto the pot letting nothing escape, and the flavors of the foods have nowhere to go but to mingle with each other. As a result, soups, stews, chilies, everything is intensely flavorful. Cuts of meat that tend to be the tastiest are also generally the toughest cuts of meat (and the least expensive too!). These meats usually need long cooking times in order to become tender, but in the pressure cooker the high pressure and temperature break down the meat creating moist, tender morsels in no time. Also, because the lid prevents steam from escaping, the moisture stays in the food. The results of pressure-cooking are juicy, tender, moist and flavorful meals. All of that in one-third of the time it would normally take. You can't beat that!

Easy

Pressure-cooking is easy. In some instances, it simply requires putting food in a pot with one cup of liquid, locking the lid in place and timing the cooking under pressure. The time it takes to cook in a pressure cooker is, for the most part, unattended time. I'm not saying you should leave the house while the pressure cooker is on, but you won't have to stand in front of it, or constantly stir or check on it. It's easy and while it looks after the main part of the meal, you can create side dishes or even just clean up the kitchen.

Energy Efficient

Because it saves time and cooks foods faster, pressure cookers use up less energy than traditional methods of cooking. Also, because the steam and heat is trapped in the pressure cooker, you will find that your kitchen remains cooler. I love this for the summer months. With a pressure cooker, you have the versatility to cook foods all year round that you might otherwise reserve just for winter. It's a shame not to have a BBQ pulled chicken sandwich just because you don't want to have your oven on for hours in the summertime.

Versatile

Many think that a pressure cooker is only for speeding up long slow braised dishes. This is far from the truth. As long as there is liquid involved either in the recipe itself or as a source for steam, you can cook it in a pressure cooker. Soups, stews, chilies, chicken dishes, leg of lamb, even seafood can all be cooked in a pressure cooker. Desserts out of the pressure cooker are probably what surprise people the most. Cheesecakes come out beautifully, poached fruit takes just one minute of cooking time, and bread puddings are delicious and easy to make in a pressure cooker. Don't be fooled into thinking a pressure cooker is a one dish pot!

Safe

Everyone seems to have heard a horror story involving a pressure cooker. Tales of marinara sauce stuck to ceilings for months, hours of cleaning split peas out of nooks and crannies, there are hundreds of such stories. The truth is that pressure cookers have improved in quality dramatically since the days of those stories, and accidents like that rarely, if ever, happen any more. Old-fashioned pressure cookers used to have a heavy lid that locked on and was weighed down with a weight to prevent the steam from escaping. There were weights of different sizes and these weights determined how much steam was released and therefore how much pressure could build up in the pot. Regulating the heat underneath the pot was the only way to regulate the pressure. These weights would jiggle on top of the cooker and start to steam, whistle and hiss when the pressure was getting too high. Neglecting the pressure cooker ended up in too much pressure building and the lid blowing off the top – hence all the horror stories.

Today's pressure cookers are better built. Stovetop cookers have safety valves built in that will release the steam in a controlled manner should the pressure get too high in the pot. Electric pressure cookers do all the monitoring for you, so all you have to do is set the time and pressure and walk away. Electric pressure cookers also have safety valves built in and steam can get blown out in a safe manner should too much pressure build up. The horror stories are things of the past.

Pressure cookers provide a lot of benefits to the cook, but pressure-cooking can also be combined with other cooking techniques for excellent results.

About Pressure Cooking

Combining Pressure-Cooking with Other Cooking Techniques

Pressure-cooking can be your sole cooking method, or it can just speed up the process of making a meal combined with a different cooking technique. Ribs, for example, can be cooked in the pressure cooker and then popped onto the grill and brushed with BBQ sauce with an excellent result. Pressure-cooked chicken wings can be finished under the broiler to get crispy edges.

The one thing that pressure-cooking doesn't do is brown your foods. So, for visual appeal as well as for flavor, it's important to brown your foods either before pressure-cooking, or after the food has been cooked. You can sear meats in a stovetop pressure cooker very easily before adding liquid and locking the lid in place, and many electric pressure cookers now have BROWN settings, which will allow you to accomplish the same thing. If your electric pressure cooker does not have a BROWN setting, simply brown the foods on the stovetop in a skillet first, add the liquid to the skillet to deglaze the pan and scrape up any brown bits that have formed on the bottom from searing the meat, and pour the entire contents into the pressure cooker along with the remaining ingredients. It's a small step that does take a little time, but it is important to the final result.

Releasing Pressure

There are two ways to reduce the pressure in a pressure cooker. The first way is called the *natural release method*. This involves simply turning an electric pressure cooker off, or removing a stovetop pressure cooker from the heat. The temperature will slowly decrease in the cooker and the pressure will come back to normal. You can tell if the pressure has dropped by checking that the pressure valve indicator has dropped and you are once again able to open the lid. (Most pressure cookers will not allow you to remove a lid when there is any pressure left inside.) If you have any question about whether or not the pressure has dropped completely, just try to release some of the pressure through the manual release valve. If steam is released through that valve, there is still pressure built inside the cooker. If nothing comes out of the valve, the pressure has dropped. The natural release method is used for most of the meats in this book for two reasons. First of all, the residual time required for the pressure to drop is part of the cooking time in the recipe. Secondly, meats tend to stay tender if the pressure is allowed to drop naturally, whereas the alternative method can toughen meats unnecessarily.

That alternative method is called the *quick-release method* and can be achieved in two ways, depending on what type of pressure cooker you are using. Most modern pressure cookers have a release valve that you can turn to release the pressure manually. Steam will shoot out the valve until the pressure has returned to normal. The second way to quick-release the pressure can only be used for stovetop pressure cookers. It involves putting the pressure cooker in the sink under cold running water. This brings the temperature (and consequently the pressure) down rapidly. Obviously, this cannot be done with electric pressure cookers. Use the quick-release method for foods that are easily over-cooked, like grains, seafood or vegetables.

Converting Recipes

Converting regular recipes into pressure cooker recipes is easy. Just make sure there is at least one cup of liquid (or the minimum amount of water suggested by your pressure cooker manufacturer) and cook the dish for one third of the time listed in the recipe.

Converting recipes for different sizes of pressure cookers can be tricky, but it doesn't need to be. The rule of thumb about pressure cookers is that you need to have at least one cup of liquid in the recipe. (Please check with your pressure cooker manual – some cookers specify different minimal amounts of liquid.) That liquid is needed to create the steam that will then create the pressure in the cooker. So, if you are decreasing the recipe, divide all the ingredients equally and then take a look at what you're left with. If there is less than one cup of liquid, increase just the liquid to one cup and leave the other quantities alone. Understand that you will probably have more sauce with your finished dish, or the final result of your cooking will be wetter than intended, but you can simply either reduce the liquid by simmering the sauce after the cooking time, or just use less of the sauce on the plate.

Here are a few tips on converting recipe sizes

- First of all, if your cooker can handle the quantity specified in the recipe, why not make the full recipe and freeze any leftovers for another occasion?

- If the liquid involved in the recipe is in proportion to the solid ingredients (such as rice or grains), do not make less than what one cup of liquid will produce.

- If you are making a roast or stew, you can decrease the meat quantity, while keeping the sauce ingredient quantities the same. Then, just use less sauce when you serve the dish.

General Tips for Pressure-Cooking

- Never fill your pressure cooker more than two-thirds full.

- Always use at least one cup of liquid (or the minimum amount of liquid suggested by your pressure cooker manufacturer).

- Check the gasket of your pressure cooker before each use to make sure that it is clean and properly in place.

- Be careful opening the lid of the pressure cooker. Even though the pressure will have dropped, the food inside will still be very hot and steam will be released.

- Let the food cool for at least 5 minutes before serving it. Foods become very hot in a pressure cooker and not only are they likely to burn if you eat them too quickly, but the flavors need a little time to blend and settle before serving.

- Because flavors can be intense in a pressure cooker, cut back on flavoring ingredients like dried herbs and spices when you are converting a regular recipe to the pressure cooker.

- If you're in a hurry and you still want to brown the meat before pressure-cooking, double up and use a second skillet on the stovetop as well as the pressure cooker to sear the meat. You'll get twice as much meat browned in the same amount of time.

- For ingredients that foam or expand in the pressure cooker (pasta, beans, grains, legumes and some fruit) be sure to only fill the cooker half full. It is also prudent to add a little oil to the cooker when cooking these ingredients to help prevent foaming.

- If the steam releasing from your pressure cooker during a quick-release starts to spit and sputter liquid, close the valve and let the pressure drop naturally.

- If your pressure cooker doesn't seem to be coming to pressure it might be because you don't have enough liquid inside. Open it up and add more liquid before trying again.

- Invest in accessories for your pressure cooker. It will expand your repertoire.

  - A rack that fits inside your pressure cooker is very important to have. I have small racks about 5-inches long by 4-inches wide. These can be used in any combination to fit most pressure cookers.

  - A 7-inch cake pan will fit inside most pressure cookers. You'll need this to cook all the bread puddings and cheesecakes.

  - A steamer basket is nice to have in a pressure cooker for steaming vegetables among other things.

- Occasionally, you might experience a "blow out" with your pressure cooker. This is not a sign of a faulty cooker, but in fact a safety mechanism. A "blow out" is when the steam will suddenly be released from the cooker, usually from the side of the lid. It occurs when too much pressure has built up in the cooker. Let the pressure drop completely, open the lid, make sure all the valves are clean and that the gasket is properly in place and try your recipe again.

- Some pressure cookers use the metric measure of kilopascals (kPa) as the unit of pressure rather than pounds per square inch (psi). HIGH pressure is usually 15 psi, which would be 103 kPa. To convert from kPa to psi, multiply the number of kPa by 0.15.

- HIGH pressure is the most commonly used pressure setting and used to be the only pressure setting available. Many pressure cookers these days have settings for LOW pressure (anywhere from 2.5 psi to 7.5 psi) and MEDIUM pressure (anywhere from 7.5 psi to 10 psi). I have not found a good use for either of these settings, except perhaps if you were cooking delicate fish or vegetables. 90% of all pressure cooker recipes, and all the recipes in this book, call for HIGH pressure.

Soups and Chilies

Beef Stock

While you don't have to start with the browning step in this recipe, it very much enhances the final result of the stock and I highly recommend it. If you're really rushed for time, however, skip step 1 and add all the ingredients to the pressure cooker at the beginning of step 2.

Serves	Prep		Cooking Time		Release Method
6 to 8 cups	**Easiest**		**HIGH 40 Minutes**		**Natural**

3 pounds beef bones and meat (any combination, but shanks are particularly good for stock, and the cheapest stew meat you can find will work well)

1 tablespoon vegetable oil

1 onion, peeled and quartered

3 carrots, scrubbed and cut into 2-inch chunks

3 stalks of celery, cut into 2-inch chunks

4 cloves garlic, smashed

2 tablespoons tomato paste

2 bay leaves

handful of fresh parsley (stems too)

few sprigs of fresh thyme

1. Pre-heat the oven to 400° F. Place all the beef bones and meat into a roasting pan and toss with the oil. Roast for 30 minutes. Toss the onion, carrots, celery and garlic with the tomato paste and add these to the roasting pan. Roast for another 15 to 20 minutes.

2. Transfer all the ingredients from the roasting pan to the pressure cooker along with the bay leaves, parsley and thyme.

3. Cover with cold water, but do not exceed the two-thirds full mark on the pressure cooker. You should add at least 6 cups of water, or as much as 8 cups. Lock the lid in place.

4. Pressure cook on HIGH for 40 minutes.

5. Let the pressure drop NATURALLY and carefully remove the lid.

6. Strain the stock into a large container and discard all the beef bones, meat and vegetables. Let the stock cool and then store in the freezer or refrigerator until needed.

TIP

When freezing stock, think ahead and use small containers (1 or 2 cups). That way you'll have usable quantities of stock ready at hand. You can even freeze stock in ice cube trays and then store the stock cubes in a freezer bag for really small quantities.

Chicken Stock

The first time I ever made chicken stock, I spent hours over it and then when I went to strain it, I poured all my beautiful stock down the drain! Don't do that! Remember to put a bowl underneath the strainer, after all it is the liquid you want to keep.

Serves	Prep	Cooking Time	Release Method
6 to 8 cups	**Easiest**	**HIGH 40 Minutes**	**Natural**

3 pounds chicken pieces (necks, backs, wings, roasted carcasses, anything)

1 onion, peeled and quartered

3 carrots, scrubbed and cut into 2-inch chunks

3 stalks of celery, cut into 2-inch chunks

4 cloves garlic, smashed

2 bay leaves

8 peppercorns

handful of fresh parsley (stems too)

few sprigs of fresh thyme

1. Place all the ingredients into the pressure cooker and cover with cold water, but do not exceed the two-thirds full mark on the pressure cooker. You should add at least 6 cups of water or as much as 8 cups. Lock the lid in place.

2. Pressure cook on HIGH for 40 minutes.

3. Let the pressure drop NATURALLY and carefully remove the lid.

4. Strain the stock into a large container and discard all the chicken pieces and vegetables. Let the stock cool and then store in the freezer or refrigerator until needed.

TIP
To remove all the fat from the stock, let it sit in the refrigerator overnight. In the morning, the fat will have congealed on the top and you'll be able to scoop it off and dispose of it.

Vegetable Stock

Store-bought vegetable stocks vary so much in their flavor, depending on the brand and what ingredients are used. With the pressure cooker you can make a stock so quickly and tailor the flavor to suit your needs.

Serves	Prep	Cooking Time	Release Method
6 to 8 cups	**Easiest**	**HIGH 12 Minutes**	**Natural**

1 tablespoon oil

1 onion, rough chopped

1 leek, cleaned and rough chopped

3 carrots, scrubbed and rough chopped

3 stalks of celery, rough chopped

4 cloves garlic, smashed

8 ounces mushrooms, halved

2 tomatoes, chopped

2 bay leaves

handful of fresh parsley (stems too)

few sprigs of fresh thyme

1. Pre-heat the pressure cooker using the BROWN setting.

2. Add the oil to the pressure cooker and then toss in the onion, leek, carrots, celery and garlic. Cook for about 5 minutes, or until the vegetables just begin to soften.

3. Add the mushrooms, tomatoes, bay leaves, parsley and thyme and the cover with cold water, but do not exceed the two-thirds full mark on the pressure cooker. You should add at least 6 cups or as much as 8 cups of water. Lock the lid in place.

4. Pressure cook on HIGH for 12 minutes.

5. Let the pressure drop NATURALLY and carefully remove the lid.

6. Strain the stock into a large container and discard all the vegetables. Let the stock cool and then store in the freezer or refrigerator until needed.

Manhattan Clam Chowder

Serves	Prep	Cooking Time	Release Method
6 to 8	**Easier**	**HIGH 8 Minutes**	**Quick**

8 strips of bacon, chopped

1 onion, finely chopped

2 carrots, finely chopped

2 ribs of celery, finely chopped

3 cloves garlic, minced

1 green bell pepper, chopped

1 teaspoon dried thyme

3 russet potatoes, peeled and chopped

2 cups clam juice

2 cups chicken stock

1 (14 ounce) can diced tomatoes

1 (14 ounce) can crushed tomatoes

2 (10 ounce) cans of baby clams, drained and rinsed

1 teaspoon salt

freshly ground black pepper

¼ cup chopped fresh parsley

1. Pre-heat the pressure cooker using the BROWN setting.

2. Cook the bacon in the cooker until most of the fat has been rendered out. Add the onion, carrot, celery, garlic, bell pepper and thyme and cook until the onion is tender.

3. Add the potatoes, clam juice, chicken stock, tomatoes and clams to the cooker. Season with salt and pepper and lock the lid in place.

4. Pressure cook on HIGH for 8 minutes.

5. Reduce the pressure with the QUICK-RELEASE method and carefully remove the lid.

6. Stir the soup well, smashing some of the potato to thicken the soup. Season to taste again with salt and pepper and stir in the parsley.

TIP

Clam juice can be found in the grocery store in the same aisle as the tinned seafood.

Corn and Potato Chowder

Serves	Prep	Cooking Time	Release Method
6	**Easier**	**HIGH 6 Minutes**	**Quick**

8 strips of bacon, chopped

1 onion, finely diced

3 carrots, finely diced

3 ribs of celery, finely diced

1 red bell pepper, finely diced

1 green bell pepper, finely diced

2 cloves garlic, minced

3 cups corn kernels (fresh or frozen)

3 cups small diced yellow potato

1 teaspoon dried thyme leaves

⅛ teaspoon cayenne pepper

1 tablespoon flour

2 teaspoons salt

freshly ground black pepper

1 quart chicken stock

1 cup half-and-half (or heavy cream)

¼ cup chopped fresh parsley

1. Pre-heat the pressure cooker using the BROWN setting.

2. Add the bacon to the pressure cooker and cook until crispy. Remove the bacon with a slotted spoon and set aside. Add the onion, carrots, celery, peppers, garlic, corn, and potato to the cooker. Continue to cook for 2 to 3 minutes and then sprinkle the thyme, cayenne, flour, salt and pepper on top. Stir well to distribute the flour evenly over the vegetables.

3. Add the chicken stock and lock the lid in place.

4. Pressure cook on HIGH for 6 minutes.

5. Reduce the pressure with the QUICK-RELEASE method and carefully remove the lid.

6. Stir the soup well to crush some of the potatoes, and add the half and half and season with salt and freshly ground black pepper. Garnish with the reserved cooked bacon and parsley and serve with a green salad and some crusty bread.

TIP

If you plan on serving this right away, half-and-half will work perfectly. If, however, you want to re-heat this soup later on, or plan on having leftovers that you might warm up again, use heavy cream – it won't separate when it gets re-heated.

Sweet Potato and Fennel Soup
with Pumpernickel Croutons

Serves	Prep	Cooking Time	Release Method
6	**Easier**	**HIGH 8 Minutes**	**Quick**

2 tablespoons butter

1 tablespoon olive oil, plus more for croutons

½ onion, chopped

1½ bulbs fennel, chopped and fronds reserved

3 sweet potatoes, peeled and chopped (about 6 cups)

4 cups water

1 small pumpernickel bread loaf, cubed

½ teaspoon salt, or more to taste

freshly ground black pepper

sour cream (optional for garnish)

1. Pre-heat the pressure cooker using the BROWN setting.

2. Add the butter and olive oil and cook the onion and fennel until tender. Add the sweet potatoes and water and lock the lid in place.

3. Pressure cook on HIGH for 8 minutes.

4. While the sweet potatoes cook, pre-heat the oven to 350° F. Toss the cubed pumpernickel with a little olive oil, salt and pepper. Spread the cubes out on a baking sheet and toast for 10 to 15 minutes or until crispy.

5. Reduce the pressure with the QUICK-RELEASE method and carefully remove the lid.

6. Using a blender or an immersion blender, purée the soup. Thin the soup with water until you've reached the desired consistency. Season to taste with salt and freshly ground black pepper. Serve with a dollop of sour cream, some of the fennel fronds and a few croutons to garnish.

TIP

When blending hot soup in a blender, be sure not to fill the blender more than half full. Hot liquids expand when puréed and steam needs to escape, so remove the cap from the blender lid and cover with a clean kitchen towel. Keep your hand on the blender lid while blending, but be careful not to get burned by any escaping steam.

Creamy Potato Leek Soup

You have a choice to use either water or chicken stock in this soup. I prefer to use water so that the flavors of the leeks and potatoes come through, but chicken stock will give you a heartier soup.

Serves	Prep	Cooking Time	Release Method
6 to 8	**Easier**	**HIGH 6 Minutes**	**Quick**

2 tablespoons butter

1 tablespoon olive oil

4 leeks, cleaned and sliced (½-inch pieces)

3 sprigs fresh thyme

1½ pounds Yukon Gold potatoes, peeled and chopped

6 cups water (or chicken stock)

2 teaspoons salt

freshly ground black pepper

1 cup heavy cream

¼ cup chopped fresh chives

1. Pre-heat the pressure cooker using the BROWN setting.

2. Melt the butter along with the olive oil in the cooker and cook the leeks for a few minutes. Add the fresh thyme, potatoes, water (or stock), salt and pepper and add enough additional water to cover the potatoes, without exceeding the two-thirds full mark on the pressure cooker. Lock the lid in place.

3. Pressure cook on HIGH for 6 minutes.

4. Reduce the pressure using the QUICK-RELEASE method and carefully remove the lid.

5. Remove the thyme sprigs. Using a blender or an immersion blender, purée the soup just until no lumps remain and the soup is smooth, without over blending.

6. Add the heavy cream and season again to taste with salt and freshly ground black pepper. If the soup needs to be thinned, just add some water until you've reached the desired consistency. Sprinkle with chopped fresh chives.

To clean leeks, cut off the dark green top of the leek where it naturally wants to break if you bend the leek from end to end. Then, slice the leek in half lengthwise and soak in cold water for 10 minutes or so, separating the leaves with your hands to remove any embedded dirt there. Dry the leeks on a clean kitchen towel and proceed with the recipe.

Sausage and Lentil Soup

I like using French green lentils for this soup because they are packed with flavor and hold their shape better than other lentils, which can turn mushy.

Serves	Prep	Cooking Time	Release Method
6 to 8	**Easiest**	**HIGH 6 Minutes**	**Natural**

1 tablespoon olive oil

1 pound hot Italian sausage, casings removed and crumbled

1 onion, finely chopped

2 carrots, finely chopped

2 ribs celery, finely chopped

2 cloves garlic, minced

½ teaspoon dried thyme

½ teaspoon dried rosemary

1 bay leaf

2 quarts chicken stock

2 cups dried French green (de Puy) lentils

salt and freshly ground black pepper

¼ cup chopped fresh parsley

1. Pre-heat the pressure cooker using the BROWN setting.

2. Add the olive oil and brown the sausage. Add the onion, carrot and celery and cook for a minute or two until the vegetables start to become tender. Add the garlic, thyme, rosemary and bay leaf and cook for another minute. Add the chicken stock and lentils, and lock the lid in place.

3. Pressure cook on HIGH for 6 minutes.

4. Let the pressure drop NATURALLY and carefully remove the lid.

5. Remove the bay leaf from the soup, season with salt and pepper, add parsley and adjust the consistency by adding more stock or water if desired.

TIP

Lentils do not need soaking, but you should look through and rinse them before using. Small stones can sometimes get mixed in, and rinsing helps wash off any stone dust.

Borscht

Few soups are as beautiful as borscht. You could use golden beets for this soup instead of red beets and still get great flavor, but you'll miss out on the spectacular garnet red color.

Serves	Prep	Cooking Time	Release Method
Serves 6	**Easier**	**HIGH 25 Minutes**	**Quick**

1 tablespoon oil

1 red onion, sliced

2 carrots, peeled and sliced

2 cloves garlic, minced

2 pounds beets, peeled and sliced

1 large russet potato, peeled and chopped

1 teaspoon dried thyme leaves

4 cups beef stock

1 tablespoon red wine vinegar

salt and freshly ground black pepper

1 cup sour cream

fresh dill (for garnish)

1. Pre-heat the pressure cooker using the BROWN setting.

2. Add the oil to the pressure cooker and cook the onion, carrots, and garlic for 2 to 3 minutes. Add the beets, potato, thyme and beef stock and lock the lid in place.

3. Pressure cook on HIGH for 25 minutes.

4. Reduce the pressure with the QUICK-RELEASE method and carefully remove the lid.

5. Using a blender or an immersion blender, purée the soup. Thin to desired consistency with water or more beef stock. Season to taste with red wine vinegar, salt and pepper. Serve with a dollop of sour cream and a sprinkling of dill.

TIP If you have a beef bone to add to this soup while it cooks, it enhances the meatiness of the soup even more. Just remember to remove it before you purée!

Split Pea and Ham Soup

My mother often used to make split pea soup for Sunday lunches when I was a kid. Split pea soup with a hunk of crusty French bread is perfect comfort food for me now.

Serves	Prep	Cooking Time	Release Method
4 to 6	**Easiest**	**HIGH 10 Minutes**	**Natural**

1 tablespoon oil

1 onion, chopped

2 stalks of celery, chopped

2 cloves garlic, minced

1 teaspoon dried thyme

1 cup dried green split peas

1 ham bone or smoked pork hock, rinsed

6 cups water

salt and freshly ground black pepper

4 ounces cooked ham (thick cut ham from the deli is perfect)

1. Pre-heat the pressure cooker using the BROWN setting.

2. Add the oil to the pressure cooker and then cook the onion, celery, garlic and thyme until the vegetables just begin to soften. Add the split peas, ham bone and the water, and lock the lid in place.

3. Pressure cook on HIGH for 10 minutes.

4. Let the pressure drop NATURALLY and carefully remove the lid.

5. Remove the ham bone from the pot and let it cool enough to pull any meat from the bone. Set the meat aside.

6. Meanwhile, using a blender or an immersion blender, purée the soup. Season to taste with salt and pepper and thin the soup with a little water if necessary. Add the cooked ham and return any meat pulled from the ham bone. Serve with some crusty bread and a green salad.

TIP

Look for pork hocks in the frozen meat section of your grocery store. The pork hock adds a great flavor to the soup, but if you can't find one, don't fret – it will still be tasty with the ham added at the end.

Navy Bean and Bacon Soup

Bean and bacon soup was one of my favorite canned soups as a kid. Making it from scratch as an adult is rewarding and takes me back to my childhood in just fifteen minutes!

Serves	Prep	Cooking Time	Release Method
6 to 8	**Easy**	**HIGH 5 + 15 Minutes**	**Quick**

2 cups dried navy beans

8 slices of bacon, chopped

1 onion, finely diced

2 carrots, finely diced

2 ribs of celery, finely diced

1 teaspoon dried thyme

½ teaspoon paprika (smoked paprika would be especially nice)

2 quarts chicken stock

1 (14 ounce) can diced tomatoes

1 tablespoon tomato paste

¾ teaspoon salt

freshly ground black pepper

1. Place the beans in the pressure cooker and add water to cover the beans by one inch. Pressure cook on HIGH for 5 minutes. Let the pressure drop NATURALLY and carefully remove the lid. Drain the beans and set aside.

2. Pre-heat the pressure cooker using the BROWN setting.

3. Add the bacon and cook until almost crispy. Remove the bacon with a slotted spoon and set aside. Add the onion, carrots, celery, thyme, and paprika to the cooker and cook until the onion starts to soften. Add the chicken stock, tomatoes and tomato paste and stir to blend well. Return the beans to the pot and season with salt and pepper. Lock the lid in place.

4. Pressure cook on HIGH for 15 minutes.

5. Reduce the pressure using the QUICK-RELEASE method and carefully remove the lid. Season to taste with salt and pepper. Using a blender, purèe just 2 cups of the soup and then return it to the cooker. Add the reserved bacon back to the soup and serve.

TIP: Smoked paprika has become much easier to find in the grocery stores since McCormick started selling and promoting it. I think it's worth a look in your local market because it adds such a nice smokiness to this soup, enhancing to the smokiness of the bacon.

Tuscan Bean Soup
with Tomatoes and Spinach

This soup is one of my favorites. With the ciabatta on the bottom, the beans and the spinach it truly is a meal all to itself. Ciabatta translates as "slipper bread" because of it's elongated flat shape. It has a crispy crust and an airy texture inside that absorbs all the flavors of the soup so well.

Serves	Prep	Cooking Time	Release Method
6 to 8	**Easy**	**HIGH 5 + 15 Minutes**	**Quick**

2 cups dried white cannellini beans

4 ounces pancetta (or bacon if you can't find pancetta)

1 onion, finely diced

3 cloves garlic, minced

1 teaspoon dried thyme

1 teaspoon dried basil

½ teaspoon dried rosemary

2 tablespoons tomato paste

3 cups chicken stock

1 (28 ounce) can whole or diced tomatoes

4 ciabatta rolls, or 1 ciabatta baguette

olive oil

5 ounces fresh baby spinach, cleaned

1 teaspoon salt

freshly ground black pepper

block of Parmesan cheese

1. Place the beans in the pressure cooker and add water to cover the beans by one inch. Pressure cook on HIGH for 5 minutes. Let the pressure drop NATURALLY and carefully remove the lid. Drain the beans and set aside.

2. Pre-heat the pressure cooker using the BROWN setting.

3. Add the pancetta (or bacon) and cook until some of the fat has been rendered out. Add the onion, garlic, thyme, basil and rosemary and cook until the onion starts to soften. Add the tomato paste and stir to blend well. Add the chicken stock, tomatoes, and return the beans to the pressure cooker. Lock the lid in place.

4. Pressure cook on HIGH for 15 minutes. While the soup is cooking, pre-heat the broiler and slice the ciabatta in half horizontally (if using a ciabatta baguette, slice into 3-inch pieces and then slice in half horizontally). Brush the cut surfaces of the ciabatta with olive oil and toast the bread under the broiler until nicely browned.

5. Reduce the pressure with the QUICK-RELEASE method and carefully remove the lid.

6. Stir the spinach into the soup and season to taste with salt and pepper. Place one toasted piece of ciabatta in each bowl. Ladle the soup over the bread and garnish by shaving Parmesan cheese on top with a vegetable peeler.

Chili con Carne

This chili includes beef and chorizo sausage – a Spanish sausage with a smoky flavor imparted by smoked red peppers. I like to use fresh chorizo in this recipe. If you can't find fresh chorizo, substitute your favorite hot Italian sausage instead.

Serves	Prep	Cooking Time	Release Method
8 to 10	**Easy**	**HIGH 5 + 15 Minutes**	**Natural**

2 cups red kidney beans

2 tablespoons vegetable oil

2 pounds ground beef

1 pound raw chorizo sausage, casing removed and crumbled

1 onion, finely chopped

2 ribs of celery, finely chopped

3 cloves garlic, minced

1 Jalapeño pepper, sliced

2 tablespoons chili powder

2 teaspoons dried oregano

½ teaspoon ground dried cumin

1 (12 ounce) bottle of lager beer

2 (28 ounce) cans whole tomatoes, drained and crushed by hand

2 tablespoons tomato paste

2 cups beef stock

2 teaspoons salt

freshly ground black pepper

½ cup chopped fresh cilantro (optional)

1. Place the beans in the pressure cooker and add enough water to cover the beans by one inch. Pressure cook on HIGH for 5 minutes. Let the pressure drop NATURALLY and carefully remove the lid. Drain the beans and set aside.

2. Pre-heat the pressure cooker using the BROWN setting.

3. Add the oil and brown the beef and chorizo in batches, setting the meat aside when brown. Add the onion, celery, garlic, Jalapeño pepper and spices, and cook for another few minutes. Add the beer, tomatoes, tomato paste, beef stock and return the beans and the browned meat to the cooker. Season with salt and pepper and lock the lid in place.

4. Pressure cook on HIGH for 15 minutes.

5. Let the pressure drop NATURALLY and carefully remove the lid.

6. Season to taste again with salt and pepper. Serve with any of several garnishes: sour cream, fresh cilantro, shredded cheese, tomato salsa.

Turkey White Bean Chili

This is my favorite ski trip chili recipe adapted for the pressure cooker. It's full of flavor and colorful, even without tomatoes.

Serves	Prep	Cooking Time	Release Method
8 to 10	**Easy**	**HIGH 5 + 20**	**Quick**

1 cup dried white beans

1 cup dried chickpeas

1 tablespoon olive oil

3 pounds ground turkey meat, white, dark or a combination of the two

2 yellow onions, chopped

2 ribs celery, chopped

2 large carrots, chopped

2 red bell peppers, chopped

2 green bell peppers, chopped

2 large cloves garlic, minced

2 teaspoons dried ground cumin

2 tablespoons chili powder

3 cups chicken stock

1 tablespoon salt

¼ cup fresh cilantro, chopped (or parsley)

Cheddar cheese, grated

sour cream

green onions, chopped

1. Place the white beans and chickpeas in the pressure cooker and add water to cover the beans by one inch. Pressure cook on HIGH for 5 minutes. Let the pressure drop NATURALLY and carefully remove the lid. Drain the beans and set aside.

2. Pre-heat the pressure cooker using the BROWN setting.

3. Add the olive oil and cook the ground turkey in batches. Set the browned meat aside and reserve. Drain off most of the fat and discard. Add the onion, celery, carrot, peppers and garlic to the pressure cooker and cook until tender. Add the dried cumin and chili powder and stir well to coat all the vegetables in the spices. Return the ground turkey, beans and chickpeas to the pressure cooker and add the chicken stock. Lock the lid in place.

4. Pressure cook on HIGH for 20 minutes.

5. Reduce the pressure with the QUICK-RELEASE method and carefully remove the lid.

6. Season with salt and stir in the fresh cilantro. Serve with a choice of garnish – Cheddar cheese, sour cream, and/or green onions.

Chipotle Chickpea Chicken Chili

Serves	Prep	Cooking Time	Release Method
8	**Easy**	**HIGH 5 + 25 Minutes**	**Quick**

2 cups dried chickpeas

1 to 2 tablespoons vegetable oil

3 pounds chicken (breast, thigh or a combination of the two), cut into bite-sized pieces

1 yellow onion, chopped

2 ribs celery, chopped

2 large carrots, chopped

3 bell peppers (any combination of red, green, yellow or orange), chopped

3 large cloves garlic, minced

2 to 3 Chipotle chilies in adobo sauce, chopped

1 teaspoon dried ground cumin

½ teaspoon paprika (smoked paprika would be nice here)

1 tablespoon chili powder

1 tablespoon salt

1 (28 ounce) can whole tomatoes

2 cups chicken stock

2 tablespoons cornmeal

¼ cup fresh cilantro, chopped (or parsley)

1. Place the chickpeas in the pressure cooker and add water to cover the chickpeas by one inch. Pressure cook on HIGH for 5 minutes. Let the pressure drop NATURALLY and carefully remove the lid. Drain the chickpeas and set aside.

2. Pre-heat the pressure cooker using the BROWN setting.

3. Add the oil and brown the chicken pieces in batches. Set the browned meat aside. Add the onion, celery, carrot, peppers and garlic to the pressure cooker and cook together over medium heat until tender. Add the chipotle chilies, dried cumin, paprika, chili powder and salt and stir well to coat all the vegetables in the spices. Return the chicken and the chickpeas to the pressure cooker, stir well and add the tomatoes and chicken stock. Lock the lid in place.

4. Pressure cook on HIGH for 25 minutes.

5. Reduce the pressure with the QUICK-RELEASE method and carefully remove the lid.

6. In a small bowl, mix the cornmeal with about ¼ cup of the liquid from the chili. Return this mixture into the chili while it is still hot and bubbling. Season again with salt to taste and stir in the fresh cilantro.

TIP

Chickpeas cooked from scratch tend to have more substance and are firmer than canned chickpeas. That's how I like them best. If you prefer canned chickpeas, however, just skip step 1 and add them in at the end of cooking when you add the cornmeal.

41

Three Bean Vegetarian Chili

Now the ingredient list for this recipe may be long, but don't let that intimidate you. They all come together to create a delicious meatless chili that will keep you coming back for another bowl without feeling too full.

Serves **6 to 8**	Prep **Easy**	Cooking Time **HIGH 5 + 15 Minutes**	Release Method **Natural**

1 cup black beans

1 cup Great Northern beans

1 cup red kidney beans

2 tablespoons olive oil

2 yellow onions, chopped

2 ribs celery, chopped

2 large carrots, sliced ¼-inch thick

3 large cloves garlic, minced

2 red bell peppers, chopped

1 green bell pepper, chopped

1 Jalapeño pepper, minced

1 teaspoon dried ground cumin

1 teaspoon dried oregano

2 tablespoons chili powder

¼ teaspoon ground cayenne pepper

1 tablespoon salt

2 tablespoons tomato paste

1 (28 ounce) can whole tomatoes

1 quart vegetable stock

1 cup corn kernels (fresh, or frozen and thawed)

1 cup peas (fresh, or frozen and thawed)

¼ cup fresh cilantro or parsley

sour cream (optional)

Cheddar cheese, grated (optional)

1. Place the beans in the pressure cooker and add water to cover the beans by one inch. Pressure cook on HIGH for 5 minutes. Let the pressure drop NATURALLY and carefully remove the lid. Drain the beans and set aside.

2. Pre-heat the pressure cooker using the BROWN setting.

3. Add the oil, onion, celery, carrots, and garlic to the pressure cooker and cook together over medium heat until tender. Add the peppers, spices and salt and continue to cook for a few minutes. Add the tomato paste, tomatoes and vegetable stock and return the beans to the pressure cooker. Lock the lid in place.

4. Pressure cook on HIGH for 15 minutes.

5. Let the pressure drop NATURALLY and carefully remove the lid.

6. Stir in the corn and peas. Season to taste with salt and stir in the fresh cilantro or parsley. Serve with sour cream and Cheddar cheese.

Chicken

Chicken Cooking Chart

The nice thing about cooking chicken in the pressure cooker is that the time it takes to cook is unattended time. If you need cooked chicken in a hurry, whether it is for a salad, pizza or sandwich, you can just pop the chicken into the cooker with the appropriate liquid, lock the lid in place and then finish making the rest of the meal. In most instances, I remove the skin of the chicken before pressure-cooking. Leaving the skin on is certainly an option, but you will need to skim a layer of fat off the top of the dish at the end (and boiled skin is rarely appealing!).

Cooking Time at HIGH Pressure

	Fresh	Frozen	Liquid Needed	Release Method
Chicken breast bone in	6 to 8 minutes	14 minutes	1 cup	Natural
Chicken breast boneless	4 minutes	10 minutes	1 cup	Natural
Chicken thigh bone in	7 minutes	14 minutes	1 cup	Natural
Chicken thigh boneless	4 minutes	10 minutes	1 cup	Natural
Cornish game hen 1 to 1½ pounds	7 minutes	14 minutes	1 cup	Natural
Turkey breast boneless, 2 to 3 pounds	20 to 25 minutes	not suggested	1½ cups	Natural
Whole chicken 3 to 4 pounds	18 minutes	not suggested	1½ cups	Natural

Basic Quick Cooked Chicken

Sometimes you just need cooked chicken for a salad, a sandwich, a pizza or just a quick dinner. Here's how you can accomplish that in just a few minutes.

Serves	Prep	Cooking Time	Release Method
6	**Easiest**	**See Chart**	**Natural**

3 to 4 pounds of chicken, whole, breasts or thighs

1½ to 2 cups chicken stock

1. Pour enough chicken stock into the cooker to cover the bottom by an inch – at least 1½ cups.

2. Place the chicken in the cooker and lock the lid in place.

3. Pressure cook on HIGH for the proper duration depending on what it is you are cooking, as listed in the cooking chart on the previous page.

4. Let the pressure drop NATURALLY and carefully remove the lid. Remove the chicken and use as needed.

TIP For a quick meal, use 2 cups of tomato sauce along with ½ cup of chicken stock, add some fresh vegetables and top with a little Parmesan cheese at the end.

BBQ Chicken Wings

Serves	Prep	Cooking Time	Release Method
6	**Easiest**	**HIGH 6 Minutes**	**Quick**

1 to 2 tablespoons vegetable oil

1 onion, finely chopped

3 cloves garlic, minced

½ teaspoon paprika

½ teaspoon chili powder

½ teaspoon dry mustard powder

¼ teaspoon ground cayenne pepper

1 cup ketchup

1 tablespoon tomato paste

2 tablespoons brown sugar

¼ cup apple cider vinegar

1 teaspoon salt

4 pounds chicken wings, trimmed

salt and freshly ground black pepper

1. Pre-heat the pressure cooker using the BROWN setting.

2. Add the oil to the cooker and cook the onion and garlic for a minute or two. Add the dry spices and continue to cook for a few minutes. Add the ketchup, tomato paste, brown sugar, cider vinegar and salt, stirring well to combine and scraping the bottom of the cooker to stir in any brown bits. Toss the chicken wings with salt and pepper and add to the cooker. Lock the lid in place.

3. Pressure cook on HIGH for 6 minutes.

4. Reduce the pressure with the QUICK-RELEASE method and carefully remove the lid.

5. For drier wings with crispy edges, remove the wings from the cooker and place them on a rack over a baking sheet. Broil for 4 to 5 minutes to get crispy edges and serve with a blue cheese dip and celery stalks.

TIP

If you find your brown sugar has hardened in its container, add a slice of apple to the container for a few hours and the brown sugar will be soft again in a jiffy.

Jerk Spiced Chicken Legs
with Rice

These chicken legs are so tasty, with a spiciness that warms rather than burns. If you'd like a spicier dish, toss a halved Habañero pepper into the cooker before pressure-cooking. Just remember to remove it before serving!

Serves	Prep	Cooking Time	Release Method
6	**Easiest**	**HIGH 8 Minutes**	**Quick**

2 teaspoons ground allspice

1 teaspoon dried thyme

1 teaspoon ground cinnamon

1 teaspoon paprika

2 teaspoons ground nutmeg

1 teaspoon ground ginger

2 teaspoons chili powder

pinch cayenne pepper

2 teaspoons salt

2 tablespoons vegetable oil

6 skinless chicken legs

1 onion, finely chopped

1½ cups long-grain white rice

2½ cups chicken stock

1 teaspoon salt

¼ cup chopped fresh cilantro (or parsley)

1. Combine the first 9 ingredients for the jerk spice rub. Rub the spice mix all over the chicken legs, or combine the spice mix and chicken legs in a plastic zipper lock bag and shake around until the legs are evenly coated. If you have time, leave the chicken with the rub for up to 30 minutes. Otherwise, proceed with the recipe.

2. Pre-heat the pressure cooker using the BROWN setting.

3. Add 1 tablespoon of the oil to the cooker and sear the chicken legs until well browned on all sides. Remove to a side plate and reserve. Add the remaining oil to the cooker and cook the onion until tender. Add the rice and stir to coat with the oil. Add the chicken stock and salt and then return the chicken legs to the cooker, placing them on top of the rice. Lock the lid in place.

4. Pressure cook on HIGH for 8 minutes.

5. Reduce the pressure with the QUICK-RELEASE method and carefully remove the lid.

6. Remove the chicken to a side plate and fluff the rice with a fork. Serve the chicken and rice together and sprinkle with chopped cilantro.

TIP Cilantro will store for up to a week in the refrigerator if you place the stems in a glass of water and cover the top with a plastic bag.

Chicken Breasts with Tomato Balsamic Sauce

This recipe starts with browning the chicken, but you don't really have to if you're in a rush. Though I like the flavor when the chicken is browned first, the sauce will cover the chicken at the end, so the appearance will not be greatly affected.

Serves	Prep	Cooking Time	Release Method
6	**Easiest**	**HIGH 8 Minutes**	**Quick**

2 tablespoons olive oil

6 boneless skinless chicken breasts

salt and freshly ground black pepper

1 onion, finely chopped

3 cloves garlic, minced

4 tomatoes, chopped

½ cup chicken stock

½ cup balsamic vinegar

¼ cup chopped fresh parsley

1. Pre-heat the pressure cooker using the BROWN setting.

2. Add the olive oil. Season the chicken with salt and pepper and sear in batches until well browned on all sides. Remove the browned chicken to a plate and set aside. Add the onion and garlic to the pressure cooker and cook for a minute or two. Add the tomatoes and stock and deglaze, scraping up any brown bits on the bottom of the cooker. Add the balsamic vinegar, return the chicken to the cooker and lock the lid in place.

3. Pressure cook on HIGH for 8 minutes.

4. Reduce the pressure with the QUICK-RELEASE method and carefully remove the lid.

5. Remove the chicken to a side plate and loosely tent with foil. Simmer the sauce in the cooker using the BROWN setting for about 6 to 8 minutes to thicken a little, and season the sauce to taste with salt and pepper. Return the chicken to the cooker to coat with the sauce and serve with white rice and fresh parsley sprinkled on top.

TIP

The trick to this recipe is to use decent balsamic vinegar – not super expensive vinegar, but vinegar that is at least 6% acidity. How can you tell? It should say "6% acidity" on the bottle. If it doesn't say it, it probably isn't.

Chicken Paprikash

I first tasted Chicken Paprikash when I worked in a restaurant in Kingston, Ontario owned by two Czechoslovakian chefs. Though Paprikash is of Hungarian origin, my two Czech chefs made a lot of eastern European dishes and did it so well. We all loved Chicken Paprikash day! This version veers slightly from the traditional by including red pepper.

Serves	Prep	Cooking Time	Release Method
6	**Easiest**	**HIGH 6 Minutes**	**Quick**

1 tablespoon vegetable oil

6 boneless skinless chicken breasts, cut into 1-inch pieces

½ onion, finely chopped

1 red bell pepper, sliced

1 clove garlic, minced

2 tablespoons paprika

1 (28 ounce) can whole tomatoes

1 cup chicken stock

2 tablespoons flour

1 cup sour cream

1 teaspoon salt

freshly ground black pepper

¼ cup chopped fresh parsley

1. Pre-heat the pressure cooker using the BROWN setting.

2. Add the oil and sear the chicken pieces until lightly brown. Remove and set aside.

3. Add the onion, bell pepper and garlic to the cooker and cook until tender. Stir in the paprika and cook for another minute. Add the tomatoes and chicken stock and stir well to scrape up any brown bits from the bottom of the cooker. Return the chicken to the pressure cooker and lock the lid in place.

4. Pressure cook on HIGH for 6 minutes.

5. Reduce the pressure with the QUICK-RELEASE method and carefully remove the lid.

6. In a small bowl, combine the flour with about ¼ cup of the hot liquid from the pressure cooker. Return this mixture to the cooker while the sauce is still hot and bubbling. Stir in the sour cream, season with salt and freshly ground black pepper and garnish with fresh parsley.

 TIP
Hungarians take their paprika seriously, and Hungarian paprika is considered to be the finest in the world. Because most of the flavor in this dish comes from paprika, I highly recommend getting the best Hungarian paprika that you can find.

Chicken with Apricots and Green Olives

This dish, with its North African spice flavor has become a favorite of many of my friends. It has a nice combination of spicy notes and sweet flavors.

Serves	Prep	Cooking Time	Release Method
4 to 6	**Easier**	**HIGH 8 Minutes**	**Quick**

2 tablespoons olive oil, divided

10 to 12 boneless skinless chicken thighs

salt and freshly ground black pepper

1 onion, finely chopped

3 carrots, sliced on the bias
(½-inch slices)

2 cloves garlic, minced

½ teaspoon ground cinnamon

½ teaspoon ground cumin

¼ teaspoon turmeric

⅛ teaspoon ground cayenne pepper

½ teaspoon ground coriander

6 ounces amber ale beer

½ cup raisins

16 dried apricot halves, halved again

½ cup pitted green olives

1 (28 ounce) can diced tomatoes

½ cup chicken stock

2 tablespoons chopped fresh parsley

1. Pre-heat the pressure cooker using the BROWN setting.

2. Add the olive oil. Season the chicken with salt and pepper and sear in batches until well browned on all sides. Remove the browned chicken to a plate and set aside.

3. Add the onion, carrot and garlic to the cooker and cook until tender. Add the dried spices and continue to cook for a minute. Pour in the beer and bring to a simmer for a minute. Add the raisins, apricot halves, olives, tomatoes and stock. Stir well and return the chicken to the cooker. Lock the lid in place.

4. Pressure cook on HIGH for 8 minutes.

5. Reduce the pressure with the QUICK-RELEASE method and carefully remove the lid.

6. Season to taste with salt and pepper and serve with fresh parsley sprinkled on top.

TIP When selecting the beer for this dish, an apricot ale is a perfect choice, enhancing the flavor of the dried apricots that are included in the dish.

Cider-Braised Chicken
with Apples and Sweet Potatoes

This is a pretty little dish, with the orange of the sweet potatoes and the green of the fresh herbs. If you're only cooking for four people, try using 8 bone-in chicken thighs – they will look more substantial on your dinner plate and cooking anything with bone-in is usually more flavorful.

Serves	Prep	Cooking Time	Release Method
4 to 6	**Easier**	**HIGH 8 Minutes**	**Quick**

1 tablespoon vegetable oil

10 to 12 boneless skinless chicken thighs

3 to 4 shallots, sliced

1 clove garlic, minced

1 large sweet potato, peeled and chopped (1½-inch chunks)

2 Granny Smith apples, peeled and chopped (1½-inch chunks)

4 sprigs fresh thyme

1 bay leaf

½ cup apple cider

½ cup chicken stock

1 tablespoon apple cider vinegar

1 cinnamon stick

1 teaspoon salt

freshly ground black pepper

1 teaspoon chopped fresh thyme leaves

1 teaspoon chopped fresh sage leaves

1. Pre-heat the pressure cooker using the BROWN setting.

2. Add the oil and brown the chicken pieces in batches, seasoning with salt and pepper. Remove the browned chicken to a plate and set aside.

3. Add the shallot and garlic to the cooker and cook until tender. Add the sweet potatoes and apples and stir to coat with the oil. Add the thyme sprigs, bay leaf, apple cider, chicken stock, apple cider vinegar and cinnamon stick. Return the chicken to the pressure cooker and lock the lid in place.

4. Pressure cook on HIGH for 8 minutes.

5. Reduce the pressure with the QUICK-RELEASE method and carefully remove the lid.

6. Remove and discard the thyme sprigs and bay leaf. Season with salt and freshly ground black pepper and garnish with the fresh herbs.

Chicken Breasts with Tarragon, Tomatoes and Cream

Tarragon is one of my favorite fresh herbs, but you can substitute almost any herb in this recipe. Basil is particularly nice.

Serves	Prep	Cooking Time	Release Method
6	**Easier**	**HIGH 8 Minutes**	**Quick**

1 tablespoon olive oil

6 boneless skinless chicken breasts

salt and freshly ground black pepper

½ onion, finely chopped

½ bulb fennel, finely chopped

1 teaspoon dried tarragon

¼ cup Pastis or Pernod (anise-flavored aperitif) (optional)

1 (28 ounce) can whole tomatoes

1 tablespoon tomato paste

¾ cup heavy cream

1½ teaspoons salt

freshly ground black pepper

¼ cup chopped fresh tarragon

1. Pre-heat the pressure cooker using the BROWN setting.

2. Add the olive oil. Season the chicken with salt and pepper, and sear the chicken until well browned on all sides. Remove the browned chicken to a plate and set aside.

3. Add the onion, fennel and dried tarragon to the pressure cooker and cook until tender. Add the Pastis and bring to a simmer. Add the tomatoes and tomato paste and scrape up any brown bits on the bottom of the cooker, breaking up the tomatoes as you stir. Return the chicken to the cooker, nestling it into the sauce and lock the lid in place.

4. Pressure cook on HIGH for 8 minutes.

5. Reduce the pressure with the QUICK-RELEASE method and remove the lid carefully.

6. Remove the chicken breasts to a side plate while you finish the sauce. Stir the heavy cream into the cooker and season to taste with salt and pepper. For a thicker sauce, use an immersion blender to purée the sauce a little – or remove half the sauce and purée in a blender, returning the purée to the sauce. Stir in the fresh tarragon. Serve with rice, mashed potatoes or over egg noodles.

TIP
If you don't have Pastis or Pernod, just leave it out or add white wine instead. Other common anise-flavored liqueurs, like Sambuca and Ouzo have sugar added to them, so do not make a good substitute here.

Chicken Breasts with Mushrooms and Sage

Serves	Prep	Cooking Time	Release Method
6	**Easier**	**HIGH 2 + 6 Minutes**	**Quick**

1 ounce dried wild mushrooms

2 cups chicken stock

6 boneless skinless chicken breasts

salt and freshly ground black pepper

flour for dredging

1 tablespoon olive oil

1 tablespoon butter

½ onion, finely chopped

1 clove garlic, minced

8 ounces brown mushrooms, sliced

½ teaspoon dried sage

1½ teaspoons salt

freshly ground black pepper

2 tablespoons chopped fresh sage

1. Place the dried mushrooms and chicken stock in the pressure cooker. Pressure cook on HIGH for 2 minutes. Reduce the pressure with the QUICK-RELEASE method and carefully remove the lid. Pour the liquid with the mushrooms into a bowl and reserve. (Alternately, you can soak the dried mushrooms in hot chicken stock for 30 minutes.)

2. Pre-heat the pressure cooker using the BROWN setting.

3. Season the chicken with salt and pepper and dredge in flour, shaking off any excess flour. Add the olive oil and butter to the cooker and brown the chicken. Remove the browned chicken to a plate and set aside. Add the onion and garlic to the cooker and cook until tender. Add the mushrooms and dried sage and continue to cook for a few minutes. Add the reserved dried mushroom-chicken stock and scrape up any brown bits on the bottom of the cooker. Return the chicken to the cooker and lock the lid in place.

4. Pressure cook on HIGH for 6 minutes.

5. Reduce the pressure with the QUICK-RELEASE method and carefully remove the lid.

6. Season to taste with salt and pepper and stir in the fresh sage. Serve over rice or mashed potatoes.

TIP

Dried mushrooms have a concentrated mushroom flavor because it takes about a pound of fresh mushrooms to make 3 ounces of dried mushrooms. If you can't find dried mushrooms, try mushroom stock, which is often available with the other store-bought stocks (or, make your own!).

Chicken with Prunes, Capers and Olives

The Silver Palate Cookbook, by Julee Rosso and Sheila Lukins, is a classic among cookbooks. Their Chicken Marbella is one of my favorites, so here it is adapted for the pressure cooker.

Serves	Prep	Cooking Time	Release Method
4 to 6	**Easier**	**HIGH 9 Minutes**	**Quick**

2 tablespoons olive oil

4 pounds chicken breasts or legs, skin removed

salt and freshly ground black pepper

1 onion, sliced

3 cloves garlic, minced

1 cup pitted prunes

½ cup pitted green olives

½ cup capers, drained and rinsed

2 teaspoons dried oregano

2 bay leaves

¼ cup brown sugar

1 cup white wine

2 tablespoons red wine vinegar

½ cup chicken stock

¼ cup chopped fresh parsley

1. Pre-heat the pressure cooker using the BROWN setting.

2. Add the olive oil. Season the chicken with salt and pepper and sear in batches until well browned on all sides. Remove the browned chicken to a plate and set aside.

3. Add the onion and garlic to the cooker and cook until tender. Add the prunes, olives, capers, oregano, bay leaves and brown sugar and continue to cook for a minute. Pour in the white wine and red wine vinegar and bring to a simmer for a minute. Add the chicken stock, return the chicken to the cooker and lock the lid in place.

4. Pressure cook on HIGH for 9 minutes.

5. Reduce the pressure with the QUICK-RELEASE method and carefully remove the lid.

6. Season to taste with salt and pepper and serve with fresh parsley sprinkled on top.

TIP Capers come either packed in salt or in a salty brine. Either way, don't forget to rinse them before you use them.

Chicken Breast with Oranges, Peppers and Basil

This is a bright, fresh and colorful dish full of flavor. It's also full of Vitamin C! If you'd prefer a thicker sauce for this dish, simply reduce the liquid at the end by simmering it for about 15 minutes while the chicken rests.

Serves	Prep	Cooking Time	Release Method
6	**Easier**	**HIGH 8 Minutes**	**Quick**

1 tablespoon olive oil

6 boneless skinless chicken breasts

salt and freshly ground black pepper

3 red bell peppers, sliced (or a mix of red, yellow and orange peppers)

1 clove garlic, sliced

1 teaspoon dried basil

1½ cups orange juice

½ cup chicken stock

3 tablespoons butter

3 oranges, peeled and segmented

fresh basil (optional for garnish)

1. Pre-heat the pressure cooker using the BROWN setting.

2. Add the olive oil and brown the chicken breasts, seasoning with salt and freshly ground black pepper. Remove the browned chicken to a plate and set aside.

3. Add the peppers, garlic and dried basil to the cooker and cook for a minute or two. Return the chicken breasts to the cooker and pour in the orange juice and chicken stock. Lock the lid in place.

4. Pressure cook on HIGH for 8 minutes.

5. Reduce the pressure using the QUICK-RELEASE method and carefully remove the lid.

6. Add the butter to the cooker and stir it into the sauce to melt. Season to taste with salt and pepper and toss in the orange segments. Serve over rice or noodles and garnish with the fresh basil.

 When slicing bell peppers, place the stem down on the counter and cut straight down the lines on the outside of the pepper. This will allow you to cut around the seed packet inside, which you'll be able to discard easily, leaving no seeds all over the cutting board.

Chicken Marsala

Though not cooked in the classic way, this speedy Chicken Marsala has all the flavors of the traditional version.

Serves	Prep	Cooking Time	Release Method
6	**Easier**	**HIGH 8 Minutes**	**Quick**

2 tablespoons olive oil

6 boneless skinless chicken breasts

salt and freshly ground black pepper

flour for dredging

1 onion, finely chopped

3 cloves garlic, minced

1 pound button mushrooms, sliced

½ cup chicken stock

½ cup Marsala wine

1 to 2 tablespoons butter

¼ cup chopped fresh parsley

1. Pre-heat the pressure cooker using the BROWN setting.

2. Add the olive oil. Season the chicken with salt and pepper, dredge lightly in flour and sear in batches until well browned on all sides. Remove the browned chicken to a plate and set aside.

3. Add the onion and garlic to the cooker and cook until tender. Add the mushrooms and continue to cook for a few minutes. Add chicken stock and Marsala wine and deglaze, scraping up any brown bits on the bottom of the cooker. Return the chicken to the cooker and lock the lid in place.

4. Pressure cook on HIGH for 8 minutes.

5. Reduce the pressure with the QUICK-RELEASE method and carefully remove the lid.

6. Remove the chicken to a side plate and loosely tent with foil. Simmer the sauce in the cooker using the BROWN setting for about 5 minutes. Turn off the heat and whisk in the butter. Season to taste with salt and pepper, return the chicken to the sauce to coat and serve with fresh parsley sprinkled on top.

Curried Chicken with Cauliflower, Peas and Basil

Serves	Prep	Cooking Time	Release Method
6	**Easier**	**HIGH 8 Minutes**	**Quick**

1 tablespoon vegetable oil

1 tablespoon butter

1 sweet onion, finely chopped

3 cloves garlic, minced

1 inch fresh gingerroot, grated

2 tablespoons curry powder

⅛ teaspoon ground cayenne pepper

2 tablespoons tomato paste

3 boneless skinless chicken breasts, cut into bite-sized pieces

1 Granny Smith apple, peeled and diced

½ cup golden raisins (or black raisins)

1 head cauliflower, cut into bite-sized pieces

2 red bell peppers, sliced

2 teaspoons salt

1½ cups chicken stock

1 cup frozen peas

1 cup unsweetened coconut milk

salt and freshly ground black pepper

¼ cup shredded fresh basil

1. Pre-heat the pressure cooker using the BROWN setting.

2. Add the oil and butter and cook the onion, garlic and ginger until tender. Add the curry powder, cayenne pepper and tomato paste, and stir to combine well. Cook for another minute to toast the spices. Add the chicken, apple, raisins, cauliflower, red pepper and salt, and stir well to coat. Pour in the chicken stock and lock the lid in place.

3. Pressure cook on HIGH for 8 minutes.

4. Reduce the pressure with the QUICK-RELEASE method and carefully remove the lid.

5. Keep the curry at a simmer using the BROWN setting. Stir the frozen peas and coconut milk into the curry and season to taste with salt and pepper. Serve with white rice and garnish with shredded basil.

TIP Gingerroot keeps very well in the freezer. Try grating it first and then freezing it in small quantities. Then you'll have grated ginger at your fingertips whenever you need it.

BBQ Pulled Chicken

You can use chicken breasts or thighs for this dish. I think it's nice to have a little of each. This recipe feeds an army and is a nice lighter version of pulled pork.

Serves	Prep	Cooking Time	Release Method
8 to 10	**Easier**	**HIGH 10 Minutes**	**Quick**

6 strips bacon, chopped

4 boneless skinless chicken breasts

6 boneless skinless chicken thighs

salt and freshly ground black pepper

1 onion, finely chopped

3 cloves garlic, minced

½ teaspoon smoked paprika

½ teaspoon chili powder

½ teaspoon dry mustard powder

¼ teaspoon ground cayenne pepper

1 cup ketchup

1 tablespoon tomato paste

2 tablespoons brown sugar

¼ cup apple cider vinegar

1 teaspoon salt

1. Pre-heat the pressure cooker using the BROWN setting.

2. Add the bacon and cook until crispy. Remove the bacon with a slotted spoon and set aside. Season the chicken with salt and pepper and add to the cooker, searing in batches until well browned on all sides. Remove the browned chicken to a plate and set aside.

3. Add the onion and garlic to the pressure cooker and cook until tender. Add the dry spices and continue to cook for a few minutes. Add the remaining ingredients, stirring well to combine and scraping the bottom of the cooker to stir in any brown bits. Return the chicken to the cooker and lock the lid in place.

4. Pressure cook on HIGH for 10 minutes.

5. Reduce the pressure with the QUICK-RELEASE method and carefully remove the lid.

6. Remove the chicken to a side plate. Once cool, shred the chicken using two forks or by hand. Add sauce to the chicken until you achieve the desired consistency. Add the reserved cooked bacon to the chicken or save it for another use.

TIP Smoked paprika is pretty easily found in the supermarket these days and gives this pulled chicken a smoky note without having to put it on the BBQ. But, if you can't find smoked paprika, regular sweet paprika will do.

Coq au Vin

If you don't want to go to the trouble of sautéing the onions and mushrooms separately, you can skip that step, but cooking them in a sauté pan is highly recommended and doesn't take any more time than the chicken takes to cook. If you are really short on time (and possibly energy), throw the onions and mushrooms in with the browned chicken along with the remaining red wine and promise you'll brown them separately "next time".

Serves	Prep	Cooking Time	Release Method
6	**Easy**	**HIGH 10 Minutes**	**Quick**

6 strips of bacon, chopped

6 chicken legs, cut into thighs with the skin removed and drumsticks

salt and freshly ground black pepper

1 onion, sliced

2 cloves garlic, minced

1 teaspoon dried thyme

1 bay leaf

1 sprig fresh rosemary

2 cups red wine, divided

½ cup chicken stock

½ cup canned diced tomatoes

4 tablespoons butter, room temperature, divided

24 pearl onions, fresh and peeled, or frozen and thawed

1 pound button mushrooms, quartered

2 tablespoons flour

¼ cup chopped fresh parsley

fresh thyme, chopped

1. Pre-heat the pressure cooker using the BROWN setting.

2. Add the bacon and cook until crisp. Remove the bacon with a slotted spoon and set aside. Season the chicken with salt and pepper and sear in batches until well browned on all sides. Remove the browned chicken to a plate and set aside.

3. Add the onion and garlic to the pressure cooker and cook until tender. Add the thyme, bay leaf and rosemary. Pour in 1½ cups of the red wine, the chicken stock and tomatoes, scraping up any brown bits on the bottom of the cooker. Return the chicken to the cooker and lock the lid in place.

4. Pressure cook on HIGH for 10 minutes. While the chicken is cooking, pre-heat a skillet over medium-high heat. Add 2 tablespoons of the butter and sauté the pearl onions until lightly brown. Add the mushrooms and continue to cook, tossing regularly. Add the remaining ½ cup of red wine and deglaze the pan, scraping up any brown bits on the bottom. Simmer on very low heat until the chicken is ready.

5. Reduce the pressure with the QUICK-RELEASE method and carefully remove the lid.

6. Transfer the chicken to a side plate while you finish the sauce. Mix the remaining 2 tablespoons of the butter with the flour, making a paste. Bring the sauce to a simmer in the pressure cooker using the BROWN setting and whisk the butter-flour paste into the liquid to thicken. Return the chicken to the cooker and add the sautéed onions and mushrooms. Season to taste with salt and pepper and sprinkle with the parsley, fresh thyme and cooked bacon.

TIP Peeling fresh pearl onions is laborious! To make it a little easier, trim the root and stem and blanch them in boiling water for a couple of minutes before peeling. To make it a lot easier, buy frozen pearl onions that are already peeled!

Beef

Beef Cooking Chart

Beef really benefits from cooking under pressure – even the toughest cuts of meat (which also happen to be the cheapest and tastiest cuts) come out tender, juicy and flavorful. I prefer to sear the beef before pressure-cooking. This creates a nice crust of flavor on the outside of the meat and definitely improves its visual appeal. As with all meats, the natural pressure release method is preferred for beef. Sometimes a quick-release will toughen the meat, whereas the natural release method allows the meat to rest and relax, which is what you should do while it is cooking!

Cooking Time at HIGH Pressure

	Fresh	Frozen	Liquid Needed	Release Method
Back ribs	25 to 30 minutes	40 minutes	1½ cups	Natural
Brisket 3 to 3 ½ pounds	55 minutes	not suggested	1½ cups	Natural
Corned beef brisket 3 to 4 pounds	55 minutes	not suggested	covered	Natural
Meatballs	5 minutes	12 minutes	1 cup	Natural
Meatloaf 2 pounds	35 minutes	not suggested	1½ cups	Natural
Roast chuck, rump, round or blade roast – 3½ to 4 pounds	50 to 55 minutes	not suggested	2 cups	Natural
Stew meat 1-inch cubes	15 minutes	25 minutes	1 cup	Natural
Short ribs	25 to 30 minutes	40 minutes	1½ cups	Natural
Veal shanks	20 to 25 minutes	not suggested	1½ cups	Natural
Veal stew meat 1-inch cubes	10 minutes	20 minutes	1 cup	Natural

Hungarian Beef Goulash

Serves	Prep	Cooking Time	Release Method
6	**Easier**	**HIGH 18 Minutes**	**Quick**

4 slices bacon, chopped

2 pounds boneless beef shank or chuck, cut into ½-inch pieces

1 onion, finely chopped

2 cloves garlic, minced

1 teaspoon caraway seeds

3 tablespoons Hungarian sweet paprika

½ cup white wine

1 (14 ounce) can diced tomatoes (fire-roasted recommended)

½ cup jarred or canned roasted red peppers, diced

1 russet potato, peeled and cut into chunks

½ cup beef stock

1½ teaspoons salt

freshly ground black pepper

½ cup chopped fresh parsley

1. Pre-heat the pressure cooker using the BROWN setting.

2. Cook the bacon until crispy, then remove and set aside to use for another purpose. Drain all but 1 tablespoon of fat from the cooker. Brown the beef in batches. Remove the browned beef to a plate and set aside.

3. Add the onion, garlic and caraway seeds to the cooker and cook for a few minutes. Add the paprika and cook for another minute or so. Add the white wine and using a wooden spoon, scrape up any brown bits that have formed on the bottom of the cooker. Add the tomatoes, roasted peppers, potato, beef stock and salt and pepper, and return the beef to the cooker. Lock the lid in place.

4. Pressure cook on HIGH for 18 minutes.

5. Reduce the pressure with the QUICK-RELEASE method and carefully remove the lid.

6. Stir the goulash well as you mix in the parsley. This will break the potato a little and thicken the goulash. Season to taste with salt and pepper and serve over mashed potatoes or egg noodles.

TIP

Just as with the Chicken Paprikash, this Hungarian Goulash gets much of its flavor from the paprika included. Hungarians take their paprika seriously, and Hungarian paprika is considered to be the finest in the world. So, once again, I highly recommend getting the best Hungarian paprika that you can find.

Sloppy Joes

Though I didn't have them often as a kid, I always enjoyed Sloppy Joe's when my mother made them, and they became a standard meal during my university days. The only reason to brown the meat in this recipe is to render some of the fat and break the ground meat apart. So, if you're in a real hurry, buy the leanest meat you can find and mix it up with the vinegar, Worcestershire sauce, tomatoes, mustard and salt before adding it to the pressure cooker.

Serves	Prep	Cooking Time	Release Method
6	**Easiest**	**HIGH 10 Minutes**	**Quick**

1 tablespoon olive oil

1½ pounds lean ground beef

1 onion, finely chopped

2 cloves garlic, minced

1 red bell pepper, finely chopped

1 tablespoon chili powder

1 tablespoon red wine vinegar

1 tablespoon Worcestershire sauce

1 (14 ounce) can crushed tomatoes

1 tablespoon tomato paste

1 teaspoon prepared mustard

1 teaspoon salt

freshly ground black pepper

6 hamburger buns, Kaiser rolls or potato rolls

scallions, sliced (optional)

1. Pre-heat the pressure cooker using the BROWN setting.

2. Add the oil and brown the beef (in batches if necessary). Set the browned meat aside and drain off all but 1 tablespoon of the fat.

3. Add the onion, garlic and bell pepper to the cooker and cook for a few minutes. Stir in the chili powder and cook for another minute or so. Add the vinegar, Worcestershire sauce, crushed tomatoes, tomato paste, mustard and salt. Stir well and return the beef to the cooker. Lock the lid in place.

4. Pressure cook on HIGH for 10 minutes.

5. Reduce the pressure with the QUICK-RELEASE method and carefully remove the lid.

6. Season to taste with salt and freshly ground black pepper and serve over the buns, garnishing with scallions if desired.

Beef Bolognese

*Few things can get my mouth watering faster than a bowl of pasta with Bolognese sauce...
especially when this version only takes 10 minutes of cooking time!*

Serves	Prep	Cooking Time	Release Method
6	**Easier**	**HIGH 10 Minutes**	**Quick**

1 pound ground beef

½ pound ground pork

½ pound ground veal (or turkey)

1 onion, finely chopped

2 cloves garlic, minced

2 carrots, finely chopped

2 ribs of celery, finely chopped

1 teaspoon dried oregano

1 bay leaf

4 sprigs fresh thyme

1 cup red wine

1 (28 ounce) can whole tomatoes

2 tablespoons tomato paste

½ cup beef stock

2 teaspoons salt

freshly ground black pepper

½ cup grated Parmesan cheese

1. Pre-heat the pressure cooker using the BROWN setting.

2. Brown beef, pork and veal in batches until the meat has broken up and the fat has been rendered. Set the browned meat aside and pour off all but 1 tablespoon of the fat.

3. Add the onion, garlic, carrots and celery to the cooker and cook for a few minutes. Stir in the dried oregano, bay leaf and fresh thyme and cook for another minute or two. Stir in the red wine, tomatoes, tomato paste, beef stock and salt and pepper. Return the meat to the cooker and lock the lid in place.

4. Pressure cook on HIGH for 10 minutes.

5. Reduce the pressure with the QUICK-RELEASE method and carefully remove the lid.

6. Season to taste with salt and freshly ground black pepper and stir in the Parmesan cheese.

TIP Whole canned tomatoes generally have a better flavor than diced tomatoes, so choose whole tomatoes and then break them up in the sauce as you stir.

Teriyaki Beef Ribs

Serves	Prep	Cooking Time	Release Method
4 to 6	**Easiest**	**HIGH 30 Minutes**	**Natural**

6 pounds beef ribs (about 20 ribs)

salt and freshly ground black pepper

1 to 2 tablespoons vegetable oil

1 cup orange juice

¼ cup soy sauce

⅔ to ¾ cup honey

4 cloves garlic, minced

2 teaspoons fresh gingerroot, minced

2 teaspoons sesame seeds, toasted

¼ teaspoon hot red pepper flakes

1. Pre-heat the pressure cooker using the BROWN setting.

2. If the ribs are in a rack, cut them into one- or two-rib sections. Season the ribs with salt and pepper. Add the oil to the cooker and brown the ribs. Remove the browned ribs to a plate and set aside.

3. Add the orange juice to the cooker and scrape up any brown bits that may have formed on the bottom. Add the remaining ingredients, return the ribs to the cooker, turning them to coat each rib in the sauce, and lock the lid in place.

4. Pressure cook on HIGH for 30 minutes.

5. Let the pressure drop NATURALLY and carefully remove the lid.

6. Remove the ribs to a resting plate and loosely tent with foil. While the ribs rest, simmer the sauce for a few minutes using the BROWN setting to let the sauce reduce a little. To serve, pour the sauce over the ribs, or return the ribs to the sauce in the cooker to coat. Serve with a cool Asian slaw.

TIP These make great appetizers if you can get your butcher to cut them across the bone into small riblettes.

Classic Pot Roast

A pot roast is a perfect meal to make in a pressure cooker. You can buy a cheap, but flavorful cut of meat and, in just an hour, serve up a tender roast with delicious gravy. The vegetables in this pot roast cook for the entire duration of the cooking time, and will be very soft at the end. If you prefer your vegetables with some bite to them, use the quick-release method to open the cooker after 35 minutes of cooking the roast, and then add the carrots and potatoes. Then return the cooker to pressure and proceed with the recipe.

Serves	Prep	Cooking Time	Release Method
6 to 8	**Easier**	**HIGH 50 Minutes**	**Natural**

3- to 3½-pound boneless chuck roast

salt and freshly ground black pepper

1 tablespoon vegetable oil

1 onion, chopped

2 stalks celery, chopped

1 cup red wine

2 cups beef stock

2 to 3 sprigs of fresh thyme

1 bay leaf

3 carrots, sliced into 2-inch slices (or use 18 baby cut carrots)

18 fingerling potatoes, left whole

2 tablespoons flour or cornstarch (optional)

¼ cup chopped fresh parsley

1. Pre-heat the pressure cooker using the BROWN setting.

2. Season the roast on all sides with salt and pepper. Add the oil to the cooker and brown the roast on all sides. Remove the browned roast to a plate and set aside.

3. Add the onion and celery to the cooker and cook for a few minutes. Pour in the red wine and using a wooden spoon, scrape up any brown bits that have formed on the bottom while you bring the liquid to a simmer. Add the beef stock, thyme and bay leaf and return the roast to the cooker. Scatter the carrots and potatoes on top and lock the lid in place.

4. Pressure cook on HIGH for 50 minutes (depending on the weight).

5. Let the pressure drop NATURALLY and carefully remove the lid.

6. Transfer the roast and vegetables to a plate and tent with foil. Bring the sauce to a simmer using the BROWN setting and let it reduce for about 10 minutes while the roast rests. If you'd like thicker gravy, mix the 2 tablespoons of flour or cornstarch with 2 tablespoons of water and stir the mixture into the sauce. Season to taste with salt and pepper and spoon the liquid and vegetables over the roast. Garnish with chopped fresh parsley.

TIP Mixing equal parts cornstarch and cold water together is called making a slurry. A slurry can be used to thicken any liquid, but the liquid must be brought to a boil in order to thicken. Don't boil it for too long, however, because the cornstarch will break down and the liquid will thin out again.

Beef Stew with Potatoes, Peas and Corn

Serves	Prep	Cooking Time	Release Method
8 to 10	**Easier**	**HIGH 15 Minutes**	**Natural**

2½ to 3 pounds beef stew meat, trimmed of fat and cut into bite-sized pieces

salt and freshly ground black pepper

1 tablespoon vegetable oil

1 onion, chopped

2 carrots, sliced ½-inch thick

1 clove garlic, minced

1 teaspoon dried thyme

1 bay leaf

3 cups beef stock

2 tablespoons Worcestershire sauce

4 Yukon Gold potatoes (or other white potato), scrubbed and cut into large chunks

1 cup frozen peas

¾ cup frozen corn kernels (or fresh kernels off the cob)

1 tablespoon butter

2 tablespoons flour

1 tablespoon chopped fresh parsley

1. Pre-heat the pressure cooker using the BROWN setting.

2. Season the beef with salt and pepper. Add the oil to the cooker and brown the beef in batches. Remove the browned meat to a plate and set aside.

3. Add the onion, carrots and garlic to the cooker and cook for a few minutes. Add the thyme and bay leaf and pour in the beef stock and Worcestershire sauce. Using a wooden spoon, scrape up any brown bits that have formed on the bottom of the cooker. Return the beef to the cooker and stir well. Scatter the potatoes on top of the beef and lock the lid in place.

4. Pressure cook on HIGH for 15 minutes.

5. Let the pressure drop NATURALLY and carefully remove the lid.

6. Add the peas and corn and let the stew simmer for a couple of minutes using the BROWN setting. Mix the butter and flour together in a small bowl and then stir this into the simmering stew to thicken it. Season to taste with salt and pepper. Sprinkle chopped parsley over the stew and serve.

TIP When you combine flour and soft butter together, the paste you create is called a *beurre manié*. A *beurre manié* is another way to thicken a liquid. When you whisk this paste into a hot liquid, the butter melts and the flour, having been blended into the butter, does not form lumps. Just bring the liquid to a boil again, and it will thicken.

Brandy Beef Stew with Beets, Parsnips and Horseradish

This is one of my favorite pot roast recipes converted into a stew for the pressure cooker. The broth stays thin, but is colored red by the beets and then pink when you add the horseradish cream.

Serves	Prep	Cooking Time	Release Method
6 to 8	**Easier**	**HIGH 15 Minutes**	**Natural**

2½ to 3 pounds beef stew meat, trimmed of fat and cut into bite-sized pieces

salt and freshly ground black pepper

1 tablespoon vegetable oil

1 onion, chopped

1 clove garlic, minced

2 to 3 sprigs of fresh thyme

½ cup brandy

2½ cups beef stock

6 beets, peeled and cut into large wedges or left whole if baby beets

5 large parsnips, peeled and chopped into 2-inch pieces

2 tablespoons lemon juice

¼ cup prepared horseradish

1 cup crème fraîche (or sour cream)

1 teaspoon chopped fresh thyme

1 tablespoon chopped fresh parsley

1. Pre-heat the pressure cooker using the BROWN setting.

2. Season the beef with salt and pepper. Add the oil to the cooker and brown the beef in batches. Remove the browned meat to a plate and set aside. Add the onion, garlic and thyme to the cooker and cook for a few minutes. Pour in the brandy and using a wooden spoon, scrape up any brown bits that have formed on the bottom of the cooker. Add the beef stock and return the beef to the cooker. Scatter the beets and parsnips on top of the beef and lock the lid in place.

3. Pressure cook on HIGH for 15 minutes. While the stew is cooking, prepare the horseradish cream by combining the lemon juice, horseradish and crème fraîche (or sour cream) in a small bowl. Mix well and season with salt and freshly ground black pepper. Set aside to serve with the finished stew.

4. Let the pressure drop NATURALLY and carefully remove the lid.

5. Season to taste with salt and pepper. Sprinkle chopped thyme and parsley over the stew and serve with a dollop of the horseradish cream in each bowl.

TIP If you're not a big fan of parsnips, this stew looks and tastes wonderful with carrots instead.

Corned Beef with Potatoes and Cabbage

The only downside to corned beef and cabbage is that most of us only have it once a year! Now that you no longer need the entire afternoon to simmer the beef, maybe you can enjoy it more often.

Serves	Prep	Cooking Time	Release Method
4 to 8 (see tip)	**Easier**	**HIGH 55 + 3 Minutes**	**Natural**

3- to 4-pound corned beef brisket

2 teaspoons black peppercorns

1 cinnamon stick, broken in half

4 allspice berries

3 whole cloves

2 bay leaves

3 cloves garlic, peeled and smashed

1 white onion, peeled and sliced

6 red potatoes, scrubbed and sliced ½-inch thick

1 head green cabbage, cut into wedges

1 to 2 tablespoons butter

1 tablespoon fresh thyme leaves

1. Place a rack in the bottom of the pressure cooker. Rinse the corned beef under cool water and then place it on the rack, fat side up. Pour water into the cooker so that it just covers the beef. Add the peppercorns, cinnamon stick, allspice berries, cloves, bay leaves, and garlic to the liquid and scatter the onions on top of the beef. Lock the lid in place.

2. Pressure cook on HIGH for 55 minutes.

3. Let the pressure drop NATURALLY and carefully remove the lid.

4. Transfer the corned beef to a resting platter and loosely tent it with foil. Add the potatoes and cabbage to the liquid in the cooker and lock the lid in place again.

5. Pressure cook on HIGH for 3 minutes.

6. Reduce the pressure with the QUICK-RELEASE method and carefully remove the lid.

7. Transfer the potatoes and cabbage to a serving dish with a slotted spoon. Toss the vegetables with the butter and fresh thyme and serve along with the corned beef, sliced against the grain into ½-inch slices.

TIP

When buying a corned beef, you'll have two different cuts to choose from. The *point cut* has more fat, but also more flavor. Estimate about a pound per person of a point cut corned beef. The *flat cut* has less fat and is easier to slice. Your yield will be higher with a flat cut, so estimate about ½ to ¾ pound of flat cut corned beef per person.

BBQ Beef Brisket

Serves	Prep	Cooking Time	Release Method
6 to 8	**Easier**	**HIGH 60 Minutes**	**Natural**

1 tablespoon vegetable oil

1 onion, chopped

4 cloves garlic, minced

1 teaspoon smoked paprika (or regular sweet paprika if you can't find smoked)

1 teaspoon chili powder

1 teaspoon dry mustard powder

½ teaspoon ground cayenne pepper

2 cups ketchup

2 tablespoons tomato paste

¼ cup brown sugar

½ cup apple cider vinegar

1 cup beef stock

1 teaspoon salt

2 potatoes, halved

3-pound beef brisket, fat trimmed

salt and freshly ground black pepper

1. Pre-heat the pressure cooker using the BROWN setting.

2. Add the oil to the cooker and cook the onion and garlic for a few minutes. Add the dried spices and continue to cook for a minute or two. Add the remaining ingredients except for the potatoes and brisket, and stir well to combine. Add the brisket to the cooker, turning it to coat it in the sauce. Push the potato halves underneath the brisket to elevate the brisket from the bottom of the cooker. (The potatoes will also help thicken the BBQ sauce in the end.) Season the beef with salt and pepper and lock the lid in place.

3. Pressure cook on HIGH for 60 minutes.

4. Let the pressure drop NATURALLY and carefully remove the lid.

5. Transfer the brisket to a resting plate and loosely tent with foil. Let the brisket rest for at least 10 minutes before slicing it into ¼-inch slices. While the brisket is resting, crush the potatoes with the back of a spoon while you bring the sauce to a simmer using the BROWN setting. Let the sauce simmer while you slice the beef. When ready to serve, either return the brisket slices to the sauce to coat, or pour the sauce over the slices. Serve on soft Kaiser rolls for a delicious sandwich.

TIP For a darker brisket with slightly charred, crispy edges, broil the cooked brisket under the broiler for a minute or two before slicing and serving.

Osso Bucco

"Osso Bucco" comes from the Italian for "bone with a hole", in reference to the veal shanks used in the dish. It's usually served over risotto Milanese, but can be made with egg noodles or potatoes as an accompaniment. To me, Osso Bucco is a special occasion meal that usually takes a few hours. Now, with the pressure cooker, it can be done in about 30 minutes!

Serves	Prep	Cooking Time	Release Method
6	**Easier**	**HIGH 20 Minutes**	**Natural**

1 to 2 tablespoons olive oil

6 large veal shanks

flour for dredging

salt and freshly ground black pepper

1 onion, finely chopped

2 carrots, sliced ¼-inch thick

2 ribs of celery, sliced ¼-inch thick

2 teaspoons fresh thyme leaves

1 bay leaf

1 teaspoon dried oregano

½ cup red wine

1 (14 ounce) can diced tomatoes

1 cup beef stock

For the *gremolata*:

zest of 1 orange, finely chopped

2 cloves garlic, minced

2 tablespoons chopped fresh parsley

1. Pre-heat the pressure cooker using the BROWN setting.

2. Season the veal shanks with salt and pepper and dredge them lightly in flour, shaking off any excess. Add the oil to the cooker and brown the shanks on all sides. Remove the browned shanks to a plate and set aside.

3. Add the onion, carrots and celery to the cooker and cook for a few minutes. Add the thyme, bay leaf and oregano and cook for another minute or so. Add the wine and using a wooden spoon, scrape up any brown bits that have formed on the bottom of the cooker while you bring the liquid to a simmer. Add the tomatoes and beef stock and return the veal to the cooker. Lock the lid in place.

4. Pressure cook on HIGH for 20 minutes. While the veal is cooking, make the *gremolata* by chopping the orange zest, garlic and parsley and combining in a small bowl.

5. Let the pressure drop NATURALLY and carefully remove the lid.

6. Season the sauce to taste with salt and pepper and serve over polenta or risotto with the *gremolata* sprinkled on top.

RARE RECIPES

PUBLISHED BY ART H

Beef Stroganoff

Serves	Prep	Cooking Time	Release Method
6 to 8	**Easier**	**HIGH 15 Minutes**	**Natural**

2 pounds round steak, cut into 1-inch pieces

salt and freshly ground black pepper

1 tablespoon vegetable oil

1 small onion, finely chopped

1 clove garlic, minced

8 ounces button mushrooms, sliced

3 to 4 sprigs fresh thyme

½ cup white wine

1 cup beef stock

two dashes Worcestershire sauce

1 cup sour cream

1 tablespoon chopped fresh parsley

paprika (for garnish)

1. Pre-heat the pressure cooker using the BROWN setting.

2. Season the beef with salt and pepper. Add the oil to the cooker and brown the beef in batches. Remove the browned beef to a plate and set aside.

3. Add the onion and garlic to the cooker and cook for a few minutes. Add the mushrooms and thyme and cook for another minute or two. Add the white wine and using a wooden spoon, scrape up any brown bits that have formed on the bottom of the cooker while you bring the liquid to a simmer. Return the beef to the cooker and stir in the beef stock and Worcestershire sauce. Lock the lid in place.

4. Pressure cook on HIGH for 15 minutes.

5. Let the pressure drop NATURALLY and carefully remove the lid.

6. Stir in the sour cream and season to taste with salt and pepper. Serve over egg noodles and sprinkle with chopped fresh parsley and paprika.

Swedish Meatballs

Serves	Prep	Cooking Time	Release Method
4 to 6	**Easy**	**HIGH 5 Minutes**	**Natural**

2 slices white bread, torn into pieces (about 1 cup)

½ cup milk

1 tablespoon vegetable oil

1 small onion, very finely chopped or grated

2 cloves garlic, minced

1 pound ground beef

1 pound ground pork

½ teaspoon ground nutmeg

½ teaspoon dry mustard powder

¼ cup finely chopped fresh parsley (plus more for garnish)

2 eggs

1 teaspoon salt

½ teaspoon freshly ground black pepper

4 tablespoons butter, divided

3 cups beef stock

4 tablespoons flour

¾ cup sour cream

1. Place the torn bread and milk in a large mixing bowl and let the bread soak while you prepare the rest of the ingredients.

2. Pre-heat the pressure cooker using the BROWN setting.

3. Add the oil and cook the onion and garlic for a few minutes. Transfer the onion and garlic to the bowl with the bread and milk. Add the ground meats, nutmeg, mustard powder, parsley, eggs, salt and pepper to the bowl and mix everything together with your hands just until everything is combined. Shape the mixture into golf ball-sized meatballs, but try not to over-handle. (A small ice cream scoop works well for this.)

4. Pre-heat the pressure cooker using the BROWN setting again. Add 2 tablespoons of the butter to the cooker and brown the meatballs on all sides. Remove the browned meatballs to a plate and set aside. (Don't burn the butter during this step. If it does burn or brown too much, wipe it out with a paper towel and add new butter.) Add the stock and return all the meatballs to the cooker, gently piling them on top of each other. Lock the lid in place.

5. Pressure cook on HIGH for 5 minutes. While the meatballs are cooking, combine the flour with the remaining butter in a small bowl to make a paste.

6. Let the pressure drop NATURALLY and carefully remove the lid.

7. Transfer the cooked meatballs to a platter and return the sauce to a simmer using the BROWN setting. Whisk the butter and flour paste into the sauce to thicken it. Stir in the sour cream and turn off the heat. Season to taste with salt and freshly ground black pepper and return the meatballs to the sauce to coat. Serve with egg noodles or mashed potatoes and some lingonberry or cranberry sauce.

Beef Bourguignon

This is another recipe like the Coq au Vin that really benefits from sautéing the mushrooms and pearl onions separately and then adding them to the dish at the end. Of course, if you don't have the time or energy for this extra step, just add the onions and mushrooms to the pot before pressure cooking.

Serves	Prep	Cooking Time	Release Method
6 to 8	**Easy**	**HIGH 15 Minutes**	**Natural**

6 ounces bacon, chopped

2½ pounds beef round or chuck roast, cut into 2-inch pieces

salt and freshly ground black pepper

2 shallots, finely chopped

3 cloves of garlic, minced

2 ribs of celery, sliced ½-inch thick

3 carrots, cut into 2-inch pieces

1 bay leaf

2 teaspoons dried thyme

2 tablespoons tomato paste

1 bottle Pinot Noir wine

1 to 2 cups beef stock

3 tablespoons butter, divided

24 pearl onions, peeled
(or use frozen, thawed)

1 pound crimini or shiitake mushrooms, stems removed and halved

1 to 2 teaspoons chopped fresh thyme leaves

2 tablespoons flour

1. Pre-heat the pressure cooker using the BROWN setting.

2. Add the bacon to the cooker and cook until almost crispy and set aside. Season the beef with salt and pepper, add to the cooker and brown in batches. Remove the browned beef to a plate and set aside.

3. Add the shallots, garlic and celery to the cooker and cook for a few minutes. Add the carrots, bay leaf, thyme and tomato paste and cook for another minute or so. Pour in the wine and using a wooden spoon, scrape up any brown bits that have formed on the bottom of the cooker. Return the beef to the cooker and add enough beef stock to just cover the other ingredients. Lock the lid in place.

4. Pressure cook on HIGH for 15 minutes. While the stew is cooking, heat a skillet over medium-high heat. Melt 1 tablespoon of butter in the pan and cook the pearl onions until they start to brown. Add the mushrooms and thyme and continue to cook until the vegetables are tender. Set aside.

5. Let the pressure drop NATURALLY and carefully remove the lid.

6. Combine the remaining two tablespoons of butter with the flour in a small bowl to make a paste. Bring the stew to a simmer using the BROWN setting and stir the butter and flour paste into the sauce to thicken it. Season to taste with salt and pepper. Return the bacon to the cooker and add the sautéed onions and mushrooms. Serve over mashed potatoes, noodles or rice and garnish with chopped parsley.

TIP

For a more elegant meal, after removing the lid of the pressure cooker in step 6, remove the beef pieces and carrots to a resting plate. Using a fine strainer, strain the sauce into a small saucepan. Bring the sauce to a simmer and whisk the butter and flour paste into the simmering liquid. Season with salt and pepper. Pour this sauce over the beef, carrots, onions, mushrooms and bacon, garnishing with chopped fresh parsley.

Ladle

Meatloaf

To make a meatloaf in the pressure cooker, you'll need a loaf or cake pan that can fit inside. While the meatloaf won't brown on top in a pressure cooker, it will cook quickly, remain very moist and the glaze at the end will add some color to the top so you won't even miss your oven.

Serves	Prep	Cooking Time	Release Method
6	**Easy**	**HIGH 35 Minutes**	**Natural**

1 cup rolled oats or fresh breadcrumbs

½ cup milk

1 tablespoon vegetable oil

1 onion, finely chopped

1 carrot, finely chopped

2 cloves garlic, minced

1 pound ground beef

½ pound ground pork

½ pound ground veal (or turkey)

½ teaspoon dried thyme

½ teaspoon dried oregano

¼ cup finely chopped fresh parsley

2 eggs

1 tablespoon Worcestershire sauce

2 teaspoons salt

½ teaspoon freshly ground black pepper

6 tablespoons ketchup

2 tablespoons brown sugar

1. Place the rolled oats and milk in a large mixing bowl and let the oats soak while you prepare the rest of the ingredients.

2. Pre-heat the pressure cooker using the BROWN setting.

3. Add the oil and then cook the onion, carrot and garlic until tender, but not browned. Transfer the vegetables to the bowl with the oats and milk. Add the ground meats, thyme, oregano, parsley, eggs, Worcestershire sauce, salt and pepper to the bowl and mix everything together with your hands just until everything is combined. Transfer the mix to a loaf pan or cake pan that will fit inside your pressure cooker and wrap well with aluminum foil. Place a rack in the bottom of the pressure cooker and place the pan on top of the rack. Pour two cups of water into the bottom of the pressure cooker and lock the lid in place.

4. Pressure cook on HIGH heat for 35 minutes. While the meatloaf is cooking, combine the ketchup and brown sugar in a small saucepan and bring to a simmer, stirring to dissolve the brown sugar.

5. Let the pressure drop NATURALLY and carefully remove the lid.

6. Remove the meatloaf from the cooker, unwrap the aluminum foil and while it is still hot, brush the top with the ketchup glaze. Let the meatloaf cool for about 10 minutes before slicing and serving.

Beef Carbonnade

Now this dish is not the prettiest meal I've seen, but what it lacks in good looks it makes up for in flavor! It takes some time to brown the meat at the beginning, but it's worth it in the end.

Serves	Prep	Cooking Time	Release Method
6 to 8	**Easy**	**HIGH 15 Minutes**	**Natural**

6 slices bacon, chopped

3 pounds beef shoulder or round, sliced into ½-inch slices

salt and freshly ground black pepper

2 white onions, sliced

2 tablespoons brown sugar

3 tablespoons red wine vinegar

1 bottle Belgian dark brown ale

1 cup beef stock

4 sprigs fresh thyme (plus more for garnish)

1 bay leaf

2 tablespoons Dijon mustard

3 slices white bread, crusts removed

1. Pre-heat the pressure cooker using the BROWN setting and heat a skillet over medium-high heat.

2. Add the bacon to the cooker and cook until crispy. Remove the bacon with a slotted spoon and set aside. While the bacon is cooking, brown the beef slices in the skillet on the stovetop, seasoning with salt and pepper. Remove the browned beef to a plate and set aside.

3. Add the onions to the skillet and cook until they start to brown. Stir in the brown sugar and caramelize the onions a little longer. Deglaze with the red wine vinegar, scraping up any brown bits that form on the bottom of the skillet with a wooden spoon.

4. Layer the beef and onions in the pressure cooker. Pour in the beer and beef stock and add the thyme and bay leaf.

5. Spread the Dijon mustard on the bread slices and lay the bread slices on top of the beef and onion mixture, mustard side down. Lock the lid in place.

6. Pressure cook on HIGH for 15 minutes.

7. Let the pressure drop NATURALLY and carefully remove the lid. Stir to break up the bread, which will help to thicken the braising liquid a little. Return the cooked bacon to the stew and season to taste with salt and pepper. Serve with boiled or mashed potatoes, using a few thyme sprigs for garnish.

Pork
and
Lamb

Pork Cooking Chart

Baby back or spare ribs are the cuts of pork that are most often cooked in a pressure cooker, but they are certainly not the only cuts of pork that are suitable for pressure-cooking and make for delicious meals. Pork loin cooks quickly and is super moist after pressure-cooking. Beautiful bone-in thick pork chops can be cooked in under 10 minutes. The biggest complaint about pork is that it can be dry, but pressure-cooking solves that problem, keeping the moisture locked in. Trim any excess fat from the pork before putting it in the cooker. Otherwise, you will have to skim off the layer of fat on top of your food at the end of cooking. I highly recommend browning the meat before pressure-cooking. Browning will not only enhance the look and flavor of your final dish, but also render some of the fat in the pork. Remember the liquid needed to cook the meat can be any liquid, not just water - use your imagination. Once again, the natural release method is better for the meat than the quick-release method which can toughen the meat.

Cooking Time at HIGH Pressure

	Fresh	Frozen	Liquid Needed	Release Method
Baby back ribs	10 minutes	not suggested	1 cup	Natural
Country-style ribs	12 to 15 minutes	not suggested	1½ cups	Natural
Meatballs	5 minutes	12 minutes	1 cup	Natural
Pork chops bone-in, 1-inch thick	6 minutes	14 minutes	1½ cups	Natural
Pork chops boneless, 1-inch thick	5 minutes	12 minutes	1½ cups	Natural
Pork loin 2 to 2½ pounds	25 minutes	not suggested	1½ cups	Natural
Sausage	5 to 7 minutes	14 minutes	1½ cups	Natural
Stew meat 1-inch cubes	15 minutes	25 minutes	1 cup	Natural

Kielbasa Sausage with Collard Greens

Kielbasa sausage can come uncooked or pre-cooked and smoked. If you are using the smoked sausage, slice the links into ½-inch slices on the bias. If, on the other hand, you choose the uncooked version, leave the links whole.

Serves	Prep	Cooking Time	Release Method
Serves 6	**Easier**	**HIGH 7 Minutes**	**Natural**

1 tablespoon olive oil

6 links kielbasa sausage

1 onion, thinly sliced

1 clove garlic, minced

1 bunch collard greens, stemmed and chopped

½ teaspoon dried thyme

1 bay leaf

1½ cups chicken stock

½ teaspoon salt

freshly ground black pepper

1. Pre-heat the pressure cooker using the BROWN setting.

2. Add the olive oil and brown the sausage. Remove the browned sausage to a plate and set aside. Add the onion, garlic, collard greens, thyme and bay leaf to the cooker and cook for a minute or two. Return the kielbasa to the cooker and add the stock. Season with salt and freshly ground black pepper and lock the lid in place.

3. Pressure cook on HIGH for 7 minutes.

4. Let the pressure drop NATURALLY and carefully remove the lid.

5. Season to taste with freshly ground black pepper. Serve with rice or over polenta.

Gumbo and Rice

There are several varieties of gumbo, a stew originating in Louisiana. Some have shellfish, while others do not. Gumbo is traditionally served over rice but in this version you cook the rice right into the gumbo, making an easy one-dish meal.

Serves	Prep	Cooking Time	Release Method
6	**Easier**	**HIGH 5 Minutes**	**Quick**

1 tablespoon olive oil

1 pound Andouille pork sausage, cut into chunks

2 boneless skinless chicken breasts, cut into ½-inch pieces

1 onion, finely chopped

2 stalks celery, finely chopped

1 green bell pepper, finely chopped

4 cloves garlic, minced

¼ teaspoon cayenne pepper

½ teaspoon dried sage

½ teaspoon dried thyme

1 bay leaf

1½ cups long-grain rice

4 cups beef stock

1 (14 ounce) can chopped tomatoes

1 tablespoon tomato paste

6 ounces smoked ham, diced

2 teaspoons Worcestershire sauce

1 teaspoon salt

4 scallions, sliced

1. Pre-heat the pressure cooker using the BROWN setting.

2. Add the olive oil and brown the Andouille sausage and chicken pieces in batches. Remove the browned meats to a plate and set aside. Add the onion, celery, green pepper and garlic to the cooker and continue to cook for a few minutes. Stir in the spices and rice and cook for a minute or so, stirring to coat the rice with the oil.

3. Add the stock, tomatoes, tomato paste, ham, Worcestershire sauce and salt. Return the browned sausage and chicken to the cooker and lock the lid in place.

4. Pressure cook on HIGH for 5 minutes.

5. Reduce the pressure with the QUICK-RELEASE method and carefully remove the lid. Stir everything together and scatter the scallions over top before serving.

TIP It's easy to add shellfish to this dish. After you release the pressure, simply nestle the shrimp into the dish and return the lid to the cooker for 3 to 5 minutes, or until the shrimp turn pink.

Italian Sausages with Pepperonata

Serves	Prep	Cooking Time	Release Method
6 to 8	**Easier**	**HIGH 7 Minutes**	**Natural**

1 tablespoon olive oil

8 links hot Italian sausage

2 onions, thinly sliced

2 cloves garlic, minced

2 red bell peppers, sliced

2 yellow bell peppers, sliced

2 green bell peppers, sliced

½ teaspoon dried thyme

1 teaspoon dried oregano

¼ teaspoon crushed red pepper flakes

1 teaspoon salt

1 cup white wine

½ cup chicken stock

freshly ground black pepper

1. Pre-heat the pressure cooker using the BROWN setting.

2. Add the olive oil and brown the sausage. Remove the browned sausage to a side plate. Add the onion, garlic, peppers, thyme, oregano, crushed red pepper flakes and salt to the cooker, and cook for a minute or two. Add the white wine and bring to a simmer. Add the stock, season with freshly ground black pepper and return the sausages to the cooker, nestling them into the vegetables. Lock the lid in place.

3. Pressure cook on HIGH for 7 minutes.

4. Let the pressure drop NATURALLY and carefully remove the lid.

5. Season to taste with freshly ground black pepper and serve with a piece of crusty bread and a salad.

Pork Chops with Creamy Mushroom Sauce

The sauce for these pork chops is brothy and flavorful. You can choose to thicken it if you like at the end of cooking, by following the tip below.

Serves	Prep	Cooking Time	Release Method
6	**Easiest**	**HIGH 6 Minutes**	**Natural**

1 tablespoon vegetable oil

6 (1-inch thick) bone-in pork loin chops

salt and freshly ground black pepper

1 onion, sliced

1 pound mushrooms, sliced

1 teaspoon dried thyme

1½ cups beef stock

½ to 1 cup heavy cream

¼ cup chopped fresh parsley

1. Pre-heat the pressure cooker using the BROWN setting.

2. Season the pork chops with salt and freshly ground black pepper. Add the oil to the cooker and brown the pork chops on both sides. Remove the browned chops to a plate and set aside.

3. Add the onion, mushrooms and thyme to the cooker and cook for a minute or two. Return the pork chops to the cooker, nestling them into the mushrooms and pour in the beef stock. Lock the lid in place.

4. Pressure cook on HIGH for 6 minutes.

5. Let the pressure drop NATURALLY and carefully remove the lid.

6. Transfer the pork chops to a resting place and loosely tent with foil. Bring the sauce to a simmer using the BROWN setting. Let the sauce simmer for 5 minutes and then pour in the heavy cream. Stir in the parsley and season to taste with salt and pepper. Spoon the mushroom sauce over the pork chops and serve.

TIP For a thicker sauce, you could either stir in 1 tablespoon of flour mixed with 1 tablespoon of soft butter, or remove a cup of the mushrooms and liquid, and purée before returning it into the sauce.

Asian Meatballs

These meatballs stay moist because of the mushrooms inside, which give off liquid as they cook.
You can use any dipping sauce you like, but Thai sweet chili sauce is easy and delicious.

Makes	Prep	Cooking Time	Release Method
18 Meatballs	**Easy**	**HIGH 5 Minutes**	**Natural**

1 large shallot, finely chopped

2 scallions, very finely chopped

2 cloves garlic, minced

1 tablespoon grated fresh gingerroot

2 teaspoons fresh thyme, finely chopped

1½ cups brown or shiitake mushrooms, very finely chopped (a food processor works well here)

2 tablespoons soy sauce

freshly ground black pepper

1 pound ground pork

½ pound ground beef

3 egg yolks

1 tablespoon vegetable oil

2 cups chicken stock

1 cup Thai sweet chili sauce (for dipping)

1. Combine the shallot, scallions, garlic, ginger, thyme, mushrooms, soy sauce, ground pepper, ground pork and beef, and egg yolks in a bowl and gently mix the ingredients together. Gently shape the mixture into golf ball-sized balls.

2. Pre-heat the pressure cooker using the BROWN setting.

3. Add some of the oil to the cooker and brown the meatballs in batches, using more oil as necessary. Remove the browned meatballs to a plate and set aside. Add the chicken stock to the pressure cooker and place either a rack or a steamer basket inside. Transfer the meatballs to the rack or steamer basket in the pressure cooker and lock the lid in place.

4. Cook on HIGH pressure for 5 minutes.

5. Let the pressure drop NATURALLY and carefully remove the lid.

6. Transfer the meatballs to a serving dish and serve with the sweet chili sauce for dipping.

TIP
Use a small ice cream scoop to quickly and uniformly shape the meatballs. Chilling the meatballs in the freezer for 15 minutes before browning helps them keep their round shape.

Country-Style Ribs with Sauerkraut

Country-style ribs are not technically ribs since they do not contain any rib bones. They are cut from the blade end of the loin, close to the shoulder and are meatier than baby back or spare ribs. Don't expect these ribs to fall apart – they will have a texture similar to pork chops, but will be super delicious.

Serves	Prep	Cooking Time	Release Method
4 to 6	**Easier**	**HIGH 15 Minutes**	**Natural**

6 slices bacon, chopped

3 pounds country-style ribs

1 onion, thinly sliced

3 Granny Smith Apples, peeled and cut into large chunks

1 pound sauerkraut, drained

½ teaspoon caraway seed

½ cup apple cider

1½ cups chicken stock

salt and freshly ground black pepper

¼ cup chopped fresh parsley

1. Pre-heat the pressure cooker using the BROWN setting.

2. Cook the bacon until crispy. Remove the bacon with a slotted spoon and set aside. Brown the ribs in the bacon fat. Remove the browned ribs to a plate and set aside. Add the onions and apples to the cooker and cook for a minute or two. Add the sauerkraut and caraway seeds and stir. Place the browned ribs on top of the sauerkraut. Add the cider and stock, season with salt and freshly ground black pepper and lock the lid in place.

3. Pressure cook on HIGH for 15 minutes.

4. Let the pressure drop NATURALLY and carefully remove the lid.

5. Remove the ribs to a resting plate and loosely tent with foil. Season the sauerkraut to taste with freshly ground black pepper, stir in the cooked bacon and parsley and serve with a piece of crusty bread and a salad.

Pork Loin with Apples and Pears

Serves	Prep	Cooking Time	Release Method
4 to 6	**Easier**	**HIGH 25 Minutes**	**Natural**

1 (2½-pound) boneless pork loin, rolled and tied

salt and freshly ground black pepper

½ teaspoon dried rosemary

1 tablespoon olive oil

½ onion, chopped

3 Granny Smith apples, peeled and cut into large chunks

3 pears, peeled and cut into large chunks

1 teaspoon dried thyme

1 cup apple cider

1 cup chicken stock

1 to 2 tablespoons brown sugar

¼ cup chopped fresh parsley

1. Pre-heat the pressure cooker using the BROWN setting.

2. Season the pork loin well with salt, pepper and dried rosemary. Add the olive oil and brown the pork loin on all sides. Remove the browned pork to a plate and set aside.

3. Add the onion, apples, pears and thyme to the cooker and cook for a minute or two. Add the cider and stock and return the pork loin to the cooker. Season with salt and freshly ground black pepper and lock the lid in place.

4. Pressure cook on HIGH for 25 minutes.

5. Let the pressure drop NATURALLY and carefully remove the lid.

6. Transfer the pork loin to a resting plate and loosely tent with foil, letting the pork rest for at least 10 minutes. While the pork rests, add the brown sugar to the fruit in the cooker and simmer the sauce using the BROWN setting until it has reduced in quantity and thickened slightly. The fruit should break down to help thicken the sauce. Season to taste with freshly ground black pepper. Stir in parsley and spoon the sauce over the sliced pork loin with a slotted spoon.

TIP There is no definitive answer about the difference between apple cider and apple juice. In many states, there is no legal distinction between the two. Some authorities, however, believe that apple juice is filtered and pasteurized while apple cider is not. Bottom line: you can use either.

Cabbage Rolls

The hardest part of making cabbage rolls is removing the outer leaves of the cabbage intact. With a pressure cooker, this task is no longer difficult. Simply cook the cored head whole for 2 minutes and the leaves will come off easily. Even though some of the inner leaves of cabbage are also used for the sauce, you'll still have some cabbage left over, so think about making a coleslaw with the remainder.

Serves	Prep	Cooking Time	Release Method
6	**Easy**	**HIGH 6 Minutes**	**Natural**

For the cabbage rolls:

2 large heads green cabbage

1 shallot, finely chopped

1 clove garlic, minced

1 pound ground pork

½ pound ground beef

1½ cups cooked rice (brown or white)

2 tablespoons tomato paste

2 tablespoons chopped fresh parsley

1½ teaspoons salt

freshly ground black pepper

For the sauce:

1 tablespoon olive oil

1 onion, finely chopped

1 (28 ounce) can diced tomatoes

1 (14 ounce) can crushed tomatoes

2 tablespoons red wine vinegar

1 tablespoon brown sugar

salt and freshly ground black pepper

chopped fresh parsley

1. Core the heads of cabbage and place them in the pressure cooker, core side down, along with enough water to cover the bottom of the pressure cooker by an inch. Pressure cook on HIGH for 2 minutes. Reduce the pressure with the QUICK-RELEASE method and carefully remove the lid. Let the cabbage cool on a towel for a minute and then carefully remove the outer leaves of the cabbage, trying not to tear them. You should get at least 6 good leaves from each head of cabbage. Cut out the thick vein from each leaf and discard. Shred half of one of the remaining cabbages and set aside.

2. Combine the shallot, garlic, pork, beef, rice, tomato paste, parsley, salt and pepper in a bowl and mix together gently. Divide the mixture into twelve portions and shape into logs about 3 inches in length. Wrap each log in a cabbage leaf, starting at the top of the leaf and folding in the sides.

3. Pre-heat the pressure cooker using the BROWN setting.

4. Add the oil to the cooker and cook the onion and shredded cabbage for a few minutes. Add the tomatoes, vinegar, brown sugar, salt and pepper and stir. Place the cabbage rolls in the sauce and lock the lid in place.

5. Pressure cook on HIGH for 6 minutes.

6. Let the pressure drop NATURALLY and carefully remove the lid.

7. Transfer the cabbage rolls to a resting plate. Season the tomato sauce to taste with salt and pepper and spoon onto a serving plate, top with the cabbage rolls, sprinkle with parsley and serve.

Lamb Cooking Chart

The most enlightening thing about cooking lamb in the pressure cooker for me was that a leg of lamb could still be medium rare in the center while the entire joint cooks quickly. Also, if you love the flavor of lamb, you'll love lamb stews in the pressure cooker. The entire stew is infused with the rich flavor of the lamb making it like no stew you've ever had before. No doubt you will notice the absence of rack of lamb and lamb shoulder chops from the cooking chart. This is because rack of lamb is a delicate cut and best prepared in an oven. Lamb shoulder chops are not suitable for pressure-cooking because they have a lot of fat that is hard to trim off. Pressure-cooking shoulder chops results in a very greasy dish, so I've not recommended them. Sear the lamb first for appearance and then let the pressure drop with the natural release method for more tender pieces of meat.

Cooking Time at HIGH Pressure

	Fresh	Frozen	Liquid Needed	Release Method
Leg of lamb 3½ to 4 pounds	45 minutes	not suggested	1½ cups	Natural
Meatballs	5 minutes	12 minutes	1 cup	Natural
Shanks	30 minutes	not suggested	1½ cups	Natural
Stew meat 1-inch cubes	15 minutes	25 minutes	1 cup	Natural

Moroccan Lamb Stew with Raisins and Almonds

This dish is a nice combination of fruity flavors and spicy notes. Served over couscous, it is not your run of the mill dinner and makes a nice change from the ordinary.

Serves	Prep	Cooking Time	Release Method
6 to 8	**Easier**	**HIGH 15 Minutes**	**Natural**

3 pounds lamb stew meat, trimmed of fat

salt and freshly ground black pepper

2 tablespoons olive oil, divided

1 onion, chopped

3 large carrots, sliced on the bias (½-inch slices)

2 cloves garlic, minced

1 tablespoon grated fresh gingerroot

½ teaspoon ground cumin

¼ teaspoon ground allspice

¼ teaspoon saffron threads, crumbled

⅛ teaspoon ground cayenne pepper

6 ounces beer (a fruity ale is perfect)

1 cup raisins

1 (28 ounce) can diced tomatoes

½ cup beef stock

zest and juice of 1 orange

2 tablespoons chopped fresh parsley

½ cup toasted slivered almonds

1. Pre-heat the pressure cooker using the BROWN setting.

2. Season the lamb with salt and pepper. Add some of the oil to the cooker and brown the lamb in batches, using more oil as necessary. Remove the browned lamb to a plate and set aside.

3. Add the onion, carrot and garlic to the cooker and cook for a few minutes. Add the ginger and dried spices and continue to cook for a minute. Pour in the beer and bring to a simmer for another minute. Return the lamb to the cooker, add the raisins, tomatoes and stock and lock the lid in place.

4. Pressure cook on HIGH for 15 minutes.

5. Let the pressure drop NATURALLY and carefully remove the lid.

6. Stir in the orange zest and juice and season to taste with salt and pepper. Sprinkle with fresh parsley and slivered almonds.

TIP Gingerroot stores very well in the freezer. Grate it first and then wrap it well in plastic wrap before freezing. Then, when you need a little ginger, you can just break off a piece and you're ready to go.

Lamb Stew Provençal

Serves	Prep	Cooking Time	Release Method
6	**Easier**	**HIGH 15 Minutes**	**Natural**

3 pounds lamb stew meat, trimmed of fat and cubed (1-inch cubes)

salt and freshly ground black pepper

2 tablespoons olive oil, divided

1 onion, finely chopped

2 cloves garlic, minced

½ cup black olives, pitted

¼ cup capers, rinsed

1 teaspoon dried basil

1 (28 ounce) can diced tomatoes

½ cup beef stock

1 bouquet garni (1 bay leaf, 6 sprigs of fresh thyme, 3 sprigs fresh parsley, 1 sprig fresh rosemary and 4 sprigs sage, tied together with kitchen twine)

2 tablespoons chopped fresh basil

1. Pre-heat the pressure cooker using the BROWN setting.

2. Season the lamb with salt and pepper. Add 1 tablespoon of the olive oil to the cooker and brown the lamb in batches, using more oil as necessary. Remove the browned lamb to a side plate and set aside.

3. Add the onion and garlic to the cooker and cook for a few minutes. Add the olives, capers and dried basil and continue to cook for a minute. Add the tomatoes, stock and bouquet garni and return the lamb to the cooker. Lock the lid in place.

4. Pressure cook on HIGH for 15 minutes.

5. Let the pressure drop NATURALLY and carefully remove the lid.

6. Remove the bouquet garni and discard. Season the stew to taste with salt and pepper and serve with fresh basil sprinkled on top.

TIP

A *bouquet garni* is a bundle of fresh herbs, tied together with twine. There's no specific recipe for which herbs need to be included, but it usually includes parsley, thyme and bay leaf. It's a great way to impart flavor to a stew, but don't forget to remove it before serving.

Greek Meatballs with Cucumber Yogurt Dip

Everyone loves meatballs! These meatballs are a little different from the usual Italian version by including some common Greek ingredients and flavors. These could be a great appetizer with the cucumber dip, or try these as a main course with the Tomato Sauce with Capers and Kalamata Olives (page 191).

Makes	Prep	Cooking Time	Release Method
18 Meatballs	**Easy**	**HIGH 5 Minutes**	**Natural**

½ cup finely minced onion

1 clove garlic, finely minced

1½ pounds ground lamb meat

3 tablespoons chopped fresh parsley

2 teaspoons chopped fresh oregano

⅔ cup black olives, finely chopped

½ cup crumbled feta cheese

½ teaspoon salt

freshly ground black pepper

1 tablespoon olive oil

1 cup beef stock

For the Dip:

1 English cucumber, finely diced

salt

2 cups whole milk yogurt

1 tablespoon fresh lemon juice

2 tablespoons chopped fresh mint

freshly ground black pepper

1. Combine the onion, garlic, lamb, parsley, oregano, olives, feta cheese, salt and pepper in a bowl and gently mix the ingredients together. Gently shape the mixture into golf ball-sized balls.

2. Pre-heat the pressure cooker using the BROWN setting.

3. Add some of the olive oil to the cooker and brown the meatballs in batches, using more oil as necessary. Remove the browned meatballs to a plate and set aside. Add the beef stock to the pressure cooker and place either a rack or a steamer basket inside. Transfer the meatballs to the rack or steamer basket in the pressure cooker and lock the lid in place.

4. Pressure cook on HIGH for 5 minutes. While the meatballs are cooking, sprinkle salt on the chopped cucumber and let it strain in a colander for about 5 minutes. Rinse off the salt and pat the cucumber dry with a clean towel. Combine the cucumber, yogurt, lemon juice, mint and pepper together and set aside.

5. Let the pressure drop NATURALLY and carefully remove the lid.

6. Serve the meatballs with the cucumber yogurt dip on the side.

Braised Lamb Shanks with Root Vegetables

Serves	Prep	Cooking Time	Release Method
6	**Easier**	**HIGH 30 + 5 Minutes**	**Natural**

1 to 2 tablespoons olive oil

6 lamb shanks

salt and freshly ground black pepper

1 onion, finely chopped

2 carrots, sliced ¼-inch thick

2 ribs of celery, sliced ¼-inch thick

2 teaspoons fresh thyme leaves

1 bay leaf

1 teaspoon dried oregano

1 cup red wine

1 cup beef stock

2 carrots, peeled and cut into 1-inch chunks

2 parsnips, cut into 1-inch chunks

2 red-skinned potatoes, scrubbed and cut into 1-inch chunks

1 rutabaga, peeled and cut into 1-inch chunks

¼ cup chopped fresh parsley

1. Pre-heat the pressure cooker using the BROWN setting.

2. Season the lamb shanks with salt and pepper. Add the oil to the cooker and brown the shanks on all sides. Remove the browned shanks to a plate and set aside. Add the onion, carrots and celery to the cooker and cook for a few minutes. Add the thyme, bay leaf and oregano and cook for another minute or so. Pour in the wine and using a wooden spoon, scrape up any brown bits that have formed on the bottom of the cooker. Add the beef stock, return the lamb shanks to the cooker and lock the lid in place.

3. Pressure cook on HIGH for 30 minutes.

4. Let the pressure drop NATURALLY and carefully remove the lid.

5. Remove the shanks to a resting plate. Strain the sauce through a sieve or colander, return the liquid back to the pressure cooker and discard the cooked vegetables. Add the carrots, parsnips, potatoes and rutabaga chunks to the cooker and lock the lid in place.

6. Pressure cook on HIGH for 5 minutes.

7. Reduce the pressure with the QUICK-RELEASE method and carefully remove the lid.

8. Season the sauce to taste with salt and pepper and add the chopped parsley. Serve the lamb shanks with the vegetables and sauce poured over top.

Leg of Lamb
with Lemon, Mint and Honey

The honey in this recipe is not a prominent flavor, but slightly sweetens the jus while the lemon and mint give a bright burst of flavor at the end. This lamb is still medium rare at the center after 45 minutes, which is perfect for me, but if you like your lamb a little more well done, increase the cooking time.

Serves	Prep	Cooking Time	Release Method
6	**Easier**	**HIGH 45 Minutes**	**Natural**

1 tablespoon olive oil

4-pound bone in leg of lamb

3 cloves garlic, sliced

2 to 3 sprigs of fresh rosemary, plus more for garnish

salt and freshly ground black pepper

1½ onions, halved and sliced

3 sprigs fresh thyme

1 bay leaf

½ cup red wine

½ cup beef stock

½ cup orange juice

3 tablespoons honey

zest of one lemon

¼ cup chopped fresh mint

1. Pre-heat the pressure cooker using the BROWN setting.

2. Prepare the lamb by making small incisions in the meat and inserting a piece of garlic and a few rosemary leaves in each incision. Season the lamb with salt and pepper. Add the olive oil to the cooker and brown the lamb on all sides. Remove the browned lamb to a plate and set aside.

3. Add the onion to the cooker and cook for a few minutes. Add the thyme, bay leaf and wine, and using a wooden spoon, scrape up any brown bits that have formed on the bottom of the cooker. Add the beef stock and orange juice and return the lamb to the cooker. Drizzle the honey over the lamb and lock the lid in place.

4. Pressure cook on HIGH for 45 minutes.

5. Let the pressure drop NATURALLY and carefully remove the lid.

6. Remove the lamb to a resting plate. Transfer the jus to a fat separator to remove the fat from the jus. Slice the lamb and ladle the onions and jus over the top. Finish by sprinkling the lemon zest and mint over everything.

TIP First things first: make sure to ask your butcher to cut the leg of lamb so that it will fit into your pressure cooker before you start preparing this dish.

Seafood

Crab and Shrimp Boil

Lemon Parsley and Garlic Steamed Clams

Mussels Marinara

Mussels with Italian Sausage and Tomato

Paella

Seafood Cooking Chart

There are not a lot of applications for fish and seafood in the pressure cooker, simply because fish and seafood by nature cook quickly. Still, it is really nice to be able to cook some seafood dishes in the pressure cooker, where you can prevent foods from splattering or steaming up your kitchen. I do enjoy locking the lid in place and having just enough time to give the kitchen a quick clean before dinner. In order not to over-cook the seafood, use the quick-release method to reduce the pressure and remember to use flavorful liquids like wines, juices and even beer instead of water.

Cooking Time at HIGH Pressure

	Fresh	Frozen	Liquid Needed	Release Method
Clams	4 minutes	not suggested	1 cup	Quick
Crab legs	4 minutes	not suggested	1 cup	Quick
Lobster tails 3½ to 4 pounds	6 minutes	10 minutes	1 cup	Quick
Mussels	4 minutes	not suggested	1 cup	Quick
Shrimp large	3 minutes	6 minutes	1 cup	Quick
White fish 1-inch thick	5 to 7 minutes	9 to 11 minutes	1 cup	Quick

Crab and Shrimp Boil

This is a quick way to make a summer favorite without having a pot of boiling water on the stovetop heating up the kitchen

Serves	Prep	Cooking Time	Release Method
6	**Easiest**	**HIGH 4 Minutes**	**Quick**

24 ounces lager beer

1 pound crab legs and claws, cut to fit into cooker

1 pound shell-on large shrimp

2 links Andouille sausage, cut into chunks (or substitute hot Italian sausage)

3 ears of corn, shucked and cut in half

2 pounds small new potatoes, scrubbed

2 lemons, halved

1 head garlic, cut in half crosswise

3 tablespoons Old Bay seasoning

chopped fresh parsley

1. Place all the ingredients in the pressure cooker and lock the lid in place.

2. Pressure cook on HIGH for 4 minutes.

3. Reduce the pressure using the QUICK-RELEASE method and carefully remove the lid.

4. Transfer the contents of the cooker to a large platter or baking sheet using a slotted spoon or tongs. Scatter parsley over the top.

Lemon Parsley and Garlic Steamed Clams

While you can use any white wine in this recipe, a Chardonnay adds a sweet note and well-rounded flavor to the clams. This recipe can be served over pasta with the broth as the sauce – call it "Pasta con Vongole" to impress your friends!

Serves	Prep	Cooking Time	Release Method
Serves 4	**Easiest**	**HIGH 4 Minutes**	**Quick**

4 pounds Littleneck clams, scrubbed

2 tablespoons olive oil

4 cloves garlic, sliced

¼ teaspoon crushed red pepper flakes

1½ cups Chardonnay wine
(or other white wine)

the zest and juice of 2 lemons

½ cup chopped fresh parsley

freshly ground black pepper

1. Discard any clams that are broken or don't close their shells when tapped.

2. Pre-heat the pressure cooker using the BROWN setting.

3. Add the olive oil and cook the garlic and crushed red pepper flakes for one to two minutes until the garlic is just starting to turn brown. Add the wine and the clams and lock the lid in place.

4. Pressure cook on HIGH for 4 minutes.

5. Reduce the pressure with the QUICK-RELEASE method and carefully remove the lid.

6. Transfer the clams to a serving dish, discarding any that did not open (do not force them open). Squeeze the lemon juice over the clams and sprinkle the parsley and lemon zest all over. Season well with freshly ground black pepper and serve with some of the steaming liquid poured over the top.

TIP If you are serving this over pasta or you would just like a richer sauce with the clams, add a tablespoon or two of butter to the broth at the end.

Mussels Marinara

Serves	Prep	Cooking Time	Release Method
4 to 6	**Easier**	**HIGH 4 Minutes**	**Quick**

4 pounds mussels

3 tablespoons olive oil

3 cloves garlic, finely chopped (about 1 tablespoon)

pinch hot red pepper flakes

½ cup white wine

2 (28 ounce) cans of crushed tomatoes

salt and freshly ground black pepper

¼ cup chopped fresh parsley or basil

1. Clean the mussels by scrubbing them with a brush under running water. Pull off the beard (the whiskery hairs protruding from the shell). Discard any mussels that are open, broken or don't close their shells when tapped.

2. Add the olive oil, garlic and hot red pepper flakes to the cold pressure cooker, and then heat the cooker using the BROWN setting. Cook gently until the garlic is fragrant, but do not brown. Add the white wine and bring to a simmer. Stir in the tomatoes and add the mussels. Lock the lid in place.

3. Pressure cook on HIGH for 4 minutes.

4. Reduce the pressure with the QUICK-RELEASE method and carefully remove the lid.

5. Season to taste with salt and pepper and stir in the fresh parsley or basil. Serve over pasta or by itself with crusty white bread to soak up the sauce.

TIP Whenever you serve a dish with mussels or clams, remember to give people a bowl into which they can discard the shells.

Mussels with Italian Sausage and Tomato

I've always loved the combination of mussels and sausage. Here they are together again. If you love spicy sausages, try using a hot Italian sausage here. I use the sweet Italian sausage, which allows more of the mussel flavor to come through.

Serves	Prep	Cooking Time	Release Method
4 to 6	**Easier**	**HIGH 4 Minutes**	**Quick**

4 pounds mussels

1 tablespoon olive oil

1 pound sweet Italian sausage, casings removed and crumbled

1 small red onion, sliced (about 1 cup)

2 cloves garlic, minced

3 tomatoes, chopped (about 2 to 2½ cups)

1½ cups white wine

2 tablespoons butter

¼ cup chopped fresh parsley

freshly ground black pepper

1. Clean the mussels by scrubbing them with a brush under running water. Pull off the beard (the whiskery hairs protruding from the shell). Discard any mussels that are open, broken or don't close their shells when tapped.

2. Pre-heat the pressure cooker using the BROWN setting.

3. Add the olive oil and brown the sausage. Add the red onion and garlic and cook for a few more minutes. Add the tomatoes, wine and the mussels and lock the lid in place.

4. Pressure cook on HIGH for 4 minutes.

5. Reduce the pressure with the QUICK-RELEASE method and carefully remove the lid.

6. Transfer the mussels to a serving dish with a slotted spoon, discarding any mussels that did not open (do not force them open). Stir the butter and parsley into the sauce and season well with freshly ground black pepper. Pour the sauce over the mussels and serve immediately with crusty bread or French fries to soak up the tasty liquid.

Paella

There are generally three different types of Paella: those with just seafood, those with just meat and mixed paellas - those with both meat and seafood. This is a mixed paella, which means there's something for everyone included!

Serves	Prep	Cooking Time	Release Method
6 to 8	**Easy**	**HIGH 4 Minutes**	**Quick**

1 tablespoon olive oil

2 links Chorizo sausage, sliced

2 boneless skinless chicken breasts, cut into ½-inch pieces

1 onion, finely chopped

1 red bell pepper, finely chopped

4 cloves garlic, minced

1½ cups short-grain rice

pinch saffron threads

½ teaspoon Spanish paprika

½ teaspoon dried oregano

3 cups chicken stock

1 (14 ounce) can diced tomatoes

12 mussels, scrubbed and de-bearded

12 clams, scrubbed

12 large raw shrimp, peeled and de-veined

salt and freshly ground black pepper

¼ cup chopped fresh parsley

5 scallions, sliced

1. Pre-heat the pressure cooker using the BROWN setting.

2. Add the olive oil and brown the sausage and chicken in batches. Remove the browned meats to a plate and set aside. Add the onion, red pepper and garlic to the cooker and continue to cook for a few minutes. Add the rice and spices, crumbling the saffron between your fingers as you add it. Stir to coat the rice with the oil and return the browned sausage and chicken to the cooker. Stir in the stock and tomatoes, drop the mussels and clams on top and lock the lid in place.

3. Pressure cook on HIGH for 4 minutes.

4. Reduce the pressure with the QUICK-RELEASE method and carefully remove the lid.

5. Add the shrimp to the cooker, tucking them into the rice and return the lid to the cooker for 3 to 5 minutes or until all the shrimp has cooked and turned bright pink. Stir everything together, adding the parsley and seasoning to taste with salt and pepper. Scatter the scallions over top before serving.

Rice, Beans and Grains

Beans, Rice and Grains Cooking Chart

Tips for cooking beans, rice and grains:

● *Beans must be soaked before cooking. You can either soak the beans in water for 4 to 8 hours (or overnight) or you can use a quick-soak method. The quick-soak method involves cooking the beans with enough water to cover by an inch for 5 minutes under HIGH pressure and then letting the pressure drop NATURALLY. Then, once drained, the beans are ready to use. Most of the recipes in this book include the quick-soak method as the first step. That gives you enough time to prepare the remaining recipe ingredients while the beans are quick-soaking.*

● *Cook no more than 3 cups of beans in a 6-quart pot.*

● *Because beans, grains and legumes can foam in the pressure cooker, be sure to only fill the cooker half full.*

● *Adding a little oil to the pot will help prevent the beans from foaming.*

● *Add salt after cooking so that the beans are not tough.*

● *While you can use a quick-release method to reduce the pressure, the skins of the beans tend to be blown apart as a result. A natural release leaves the beans intact and more attractive.*

● *1 cup uncooked white rice = 3 cups cooked rice*

● *1 cup uncooked brown rice = 4 cups cooked rice*

1 Cup	Cooking Time at HIGH Pressure	Liquid Needed per cup	Release Method
Brown Rice	12 to 15 minutes	2 cups	Natural
White Rice long grain	4 minutes	1½ cups	Quick
White Rice short grain	7 minutes	2⅔ cups	Quick
Wild rice	20 minutes	4 cups	Quick
Black beans quick-soaked	15 to 18 minutes	covered	Natural
Cannellini beans quick-soaked	15 minutes	covered	Natural
Chickpeas quick-soaked	16 minutes	covered	Natural
Great Northern beans quick-soaked	15 minutes	covered	Natural
Kidney beans quick-soaked	15 minutes	covered	Natural
Navy beans quick-soaked	15 to 18 minutes	covered	Natural
Pinto beans quick-soaked	12 minutes	covered	Natural
White beans quick-soaked	15 minutes	covered	Natural
Barley	20 minutes	4 cups	Quick
Bulgur	6 minutes	2 cups	Quick
Farro	16 to 18 minutes	3 cups	Quick
Polenta	5 minutes	3 cups	Quick
Quinoa	5 minutes	1⅔ cups	Quick
Lentils French green	8 minutes	covered	Quick
Split peas	10 minutes	covered	Natural

Indian Spiced Basmati Rice

To make rice with a twist, here's a simple recipe. This would pair nicely with the Curried Chicken with Cauliflower, Peas and Basil (page 65).

Serves	Prep	Cooking Time	Release Method
4 to 6	**Easiest**	**HIGH 4 Minutes**	**Quick**

1 tablespoon vegetable oil

1 tablespoon butter

½ onion, finely chopped

2 cloves garlic, minced

2 cardamom pods

2 whole cloves

1 cinnamon stick, broken in half

1 teaspoon dried cumin seeds

¼ teaspoon turmeric

2 cups basmati rice

2 teaspoons salt

freshly ground black pepper

3 cups water

1. Pre-heat the pressure cooker using the BROWN setting.

2. Add the oil and butter and cook the onion, garlic and spices until the onion is tender and the spices are fragrant. Stir in the rice, salt and pepper. Add the water and lock the lid in place.

3. Pressure cook on HIGH for 4 minutes.

4. Reduce the pressure with the QUICK-RELEASE method and carefully remove the lid.

5. Fluff the rice with a fork, remove the cinnamon sticks, cloves and cardamom pods and serve.

Risotto with Butternut Squash and Sage

Traditionally, risotto can take about 30 minutes of stirring over a stovetop. The pressure cooker makes quick work of the task with a cook time of only 7 minutes!

Serves	Prep	Cooking Time	Release Method
6	**Easiest**	**HIGH 7 Minutes**	**Quick**

1 tablespoon olive oil

½ cup chopped shallots
(about 1 large shallot)

2 cloves garlic, minced

1 small butternut squash, peeled
and cut into ½-inch dice

2 tablespoons fresh sage, chopped

1½ cups Arborio or Carnaroli rice

½ cup white wine

3½ cups chicken or vegetable stock

¼ cup grated Parmesan cheese

juice of half a lemon

2 teaspoons salt

freshly ground black pepper

¼ cup chopped fresh parsley

1. Pre-heat the pressure cooker using the BROWN setting.

2. Add the oil and cook the shallots and garlic for a few minutes. Add the butternut squash and sage and cook for another minute or two. Add the rice, wine and stock, stir and lock the lid in place.

3. Pressure cook on HIGH for 7 minutes.

4. Reduce the pressure with the QUICK-RELEASE method and carefully remove the lid.

5. Stir in the cheese and season to taste with lemon juice, salt and pepper. Sprinkle the chopped parsley on top.

TIP You can use either Arborio or Carnaroli rice for risotto. The lesser-known Carnaroli rice is a medium-grained rice with higher starch content, firmer texture and a longer grain than Arborio rice, which is a short-grain rice.

Wild Mushroom and Lemon Risotto

In the same manner as a chain is only as strong as its weakest link, this risotto will be only as tasty as the mushrooms you use, so buy the nicest mushrooms you can find.

Serves	Prep	Cooking Time	Release Method
4 to 6	**Easiest**	**HIGH 7 Minutes**	**Quick**

2 tablespoons olive oil

½ cup chopped shallots (about 1 large shallot)

2 cloves garlic, minced

1 pound assorted wild mushrooms (crimini, shiitake, oyster or portobellos, brown or even button)

2 tablespoons fresh thyme, chopped

1½ cups Arborio or Carnaroli rice

½ cup white wine

3½ cups chicken or vegetable stock

¼ cup grated Parmesan cheese

1 tablespoon lemon zest (plus more for garnish if desired)

1 tablespoon fresh lemon juice

¼ cup chopped fresh parsley

2 teaspoons salt

freshly ground black pepper

1. Pre-heat the pressure cooker using the BROWN setting.

2. Add the oil and cook the shallots and garlic for a few minutes. Add the mushrooms and thyme and cook for another few minutes, browning lightly. Add the rice, wine and stock, stir and lock the lid in place.

3. Pressure cook on HIGH for 7 minutes.

4. Reduce the pressure with the QUICK-RELEASE method, and carefully remove the lid.

5. Stir in the cheese, lemon zest, lemon juice and parsley and season to taste with salt and pepper.

Spanish Rice

Don't rush the first step of this recipe. Browning the rice is the most important step in Spanish rice, giving a nutty, toasted flavor to the final dish.

Serves	Prep	Cooking Time	Release Method
4 to 6	**Easiest**	**HIGH 4 Minutes**	**Quick**

1 tablespoon olive oil

2 cups long-grain rice

1 onion, finely chopped

1 green pepper, finely chopped

2 cloves garlic, minced

1 teaspoon dried oregano

½ teaspoon Spanish paprika

1 (28 ounce) can chopped tomatoes, drained

2¼ cups chicken stock

1 teaspoon salt

¼ cup chopped fresh parsley or cilantro

1. Pre-heat the pressure cooker using the BROWN setting.

2. Add the olive oil and cook the rice until it starts to take on a golden color. Add the onion, green pepper, garlic, oregano and paprika and cook for a few minutes.

3. Add the drained tomatoes, chicken stock and salt and lock the lid in place.

4. Pressure cook on HIGH for 4 minutes.

5. Reduce the pressure with the QUICK-RELEASE method and carefully remove the lid.

6. Fluff the rice with a fork, mixing in the parsley or cilantro and transfer to a serving dish.

Tomato Dill Rice with Shrimp

This dish is light and easy, serving 4 as a main meal or 6 as a side dish.

Serves	Prep	Cooking Time	Release Method
4 to 6	**Easiest**	**HIGH 4 Minutes**	**Quick**

1 tablespoon olive oil

½ onion, finely chopped

1 clove garlic, minced

2 cups long-grain rice

1 (14 ounce) can diced tomatoes, drained

20 large shrimp, peeled and de-veined

1½ teaspoons salt

freshly ground black pepper

3 cups water

½ cup chopped fresh dill

1 lemon (optional)

1. Pre-heat the pressure cooker using the BROWN setting.

2. Add the oil and cook the onion and garlic for a few minutes. Stir in the rice, tomatoes, shrimp, salt and pepper. Add the water and lock the lid in place.

3. Pressure cook on HIGH for 4 minutes.

4. Reduce the pressure with the QUICK-RELEASE method and carefully remove the lid.

5. Fluff the rice with a fork while you mix in the dill and season to taste with salt and pepper. Replace the lid and let the rice steam for 5 minutes before serving with lemon pieces (if desired).

Quinoa with Cinnamon and Raisins

Quinoa is actually a seed rather than a grain, and is a relative of the leafy greens and beet family. It is high in protein and a good source of dietary fiber, but don't let that fool you ... it's tasty too!

Serves **6**	Prep **Easiest**	Cooking Time **HIGH 5 Minutes**	Release Method **Quick**

1 tablespoon olive oil

2 shallots, finely chopped

1½ cups quinoa

2 cinnamon sticks, broken into 4 pieces

1 cup raisins

2½ cups water

1 teaspoon salt

¼ cup chopped fresh parsley or cilantro

freshly ground black pepper

1. Pre-heat the pressure cooker using the BROWN setting.

2. Add the oil and cook the shallots for a few minutes. Stir in the quinoa and cinnamon sticks and cook for another minute or two. Add the raisins, water and salt and lock the lid in place.

3. Pressure cook on HIGH for 5 minutes.

4. Reduce the pressure with the QUICK-RELEASE method and carefully remove the lid.

5. Add the parsley and fluff the quinoa with a fork. Season to taste with salt and freshly ground black pepper and serve.

Polenta with Parmesan Cheese and Pancetta

Polenta is such a nice accompaniment to so many of the dishes in this book, but it would be especially nice with the Osso Bucco on page 86.

Serves	Prep	Cooking Time	Release Method
6	**Easiest**	**HIGH 5 Minutes**	**Quick**

8 slices of pancetta (or 6 slices of bacon), chopped

4½ cups water (or stock)

1½ cups polenta

1 teaspoon salt

1 tablespoon olive oil

2 tablespoons butter

½ cup grated Parmesan cheese

freshly ground black pepper

1. Pre-heat the pressure cooker using the BROWN setting.

2. Add the pancetta and cook until crispy. Remove the pancetta with a slotted spoon and set aside. Add the water to the cooker and bring to a boil. Stir in the polenta and salt and drizzle the olive oil on top. Lock the lid in place.

3. Pressure cook on HIGH For 5 minutes.

4. Reduce the pressure with the QUICK-RELEASE method and carefully remove the lid.

5. Stir in the butter and Parmesan cheese. Season to taste with salt and freshly ground black pepper and stir in the cooked pancetta.

TIP If you have any leftover polenta, pour the remainder into a baking dish and chill it in the fridge. Then slice it into pieces and grill it or sauté it as an accompaniment to another meal.

Tabbouleh
(or Bulgur Salad with Cucumber, Tomato and Herbs)

Tabbouleh is a Middle Eastern salad made with a lot of fresh herbs. That's why I've given you quantities in bunches below. Bulgur is a form of whole wheat that is high in fiber and low on the glycemic index. This salad makes a perfect summer lunch with a piece of fresh pita bread, or is a great side dish to some grilled kebabs.

Serves	Prep	Cooking Time	Release Method
6 to 8	**Easiest**	**HIGH 6 Minutes**	**Quick**

1½ cups bulgur

3 cups water

1 teaspoon salt

1 English cucumber, diced ¼-inch

3 tomatoes, diced ¼-inch

1½ cups chopped fresh parsley
(about 1 – 2 bunches)

1½ cups chopped fresh mint
(1 large bunch)

6 tablespoons fresh lemon juice
(about 2 large lemons)

6 tablespoons extra virgin olive oil

salt and freshly ground black pepper

1. Combine the bulgur, water and salt in the pressure cooker and lock the lid in place.

2. Pressure cook on HIGH For 6 minutes. While the bulgur is cooking, combine the cucumber, tomatoes, parsley and mint in a large bowl.

3. Reduce the pressure with the QUICK-RELEASE method and carefully remove the lid.

4. Spread the bulgur out on a baking sheet and let it cool.

5. When it is cool, add the bulgur to the bowl with the tomato mixture and stir well. Add the lemon juice and olive oil, mix well and season with salt and freshly ground black pepper.

TIP Bulgur is different from cracked wheat in that it is par-boiled.

Wild Rice with Mushrooms and Peas

Wild rice is a grass rather than a grain, and on the stovetop it can take 40 to 50 minutes to cook. The pressure cooker brings that time down to 20 minutes! How's that for wild?

Serves **4 to 6**	Prep **Easiest**	Cooking Time **HIGH 20 Minutes**	Release Method **Quick**

1 tablespoon olive oil

½ onion, finely chopped

8 ounces brown mushrooms, sliced

2 teaspoons chopped fresh thyme

1 cup wild rice

1½ teaspoons salt

freshly ground black pepper

3 cups water or chicken stock

¾ cup frozen peas

1. Pre-heat the pressure cooker using the BROWN setting.

2. Add the oil and cook the onion for a few minutes. Add the mushrooms and thyme and cook for another minute or so. Stir in the rice, salt and pepper, add the water or chicken stock and lock the lid in place.

3. Pressure cook on HIGH for 20 minutes.

4. Reduce the pressure with the QUICK-RELEASE method and carefully remove the lid.

5. Immediately add the peas and stir them into the rice. Return the lid to the pressure cooker and let it sit for a minute. Then, strain the rice (there should be up to a cup of extra liquid) and serve.

Wild Rice with Pecans, Cranberries and Parsley

Serves	Prep	Cooking Time	Release Method
4 to 6	**Easiest**	**HIGH 20 Minutes**	**Quick**

1 tablespoon olive oil

½ onion, finely chopped

2 teaspoons chopped fresh thyme

½ cup dried cranberries

1 cup wild rice

½ teaspoon salt

freshly ground black pepper

3 cups chicken stock

¾ cup chopped pecans

1 tablespoon red wine vinegar

¼ cup chopped fresh parsley

extra virgin olive oil

1. Pre-heat the pressure cooker using the BROWN setting.

2. Add the oil and cook the onion for a few minutes. Stir in the thyme, cranberries, rice, salt and pepper, add the chicken stock and lock the lid in place.

3. Pressure cook on HIGH for 20 minutes. While the rice is cooking, toast the pecans in the oven at 350° F or in a dry skillet on the stovetop until lightly brown and crunchy.

4. Reduce the pressure with the QUICK-RELEASE method and carefully remove the lid.

5. Strain the rice with a fine sieve or transfer the rice to a serving bowl with a slotted spoon. Immediately toss in the vinegar, toasted pecans and parsley and drizzle with extra virgin olive oil.

TIP This dish is also quite nice served cold as a salad.

Lentils with Tomatoes, Fresh Herbs and Feta

There are so many great things to say about lentils. They are the seeds of a bush in the pulse family and they are high in protein, iron and dietary fiber. They can be served warm or cold and also make delicious soup. They come in many different colors, but my favorite by far are the French green lentils also known as lentilles du Puy.

Serves	Prep	Cooking Time	Release Method
6	**Easier**	**HIGH 8 Minutes**	**Quick**

1 tablespoon olive oil

1 onion, finely chopped

1 carrot, finely chopped

2 cups French green lentils (du Puy)

1 (28 ounce) can diced tomatoes

2 cups water

2 teaspoons salt

freshly ground black pepper

½ cup chopped fresh parsley

¼ cup chopped fresh mint

2 tablespoons chopped fresh chives

2 tablespoons extra virgin olive oil

1 teaspoon red wine vinegar

4 ounces feta cheese, crumbled

1. Pre-heat the pressure cooker using the BROWN setting.

2. Add the olive oil and cook the onion and carrot for a few minutes. Add the lentils and tomatoes and stir. Pour in the water and season with salt and freshly ground black pepper. Lock the lid in place.

3. Pressure cook on HIGH for 8 minutes.

4. Reduce the pressure with the QUICK-RELEASE method and carefully remove the lid.

5. Season to taste with salt and pepper again and stir in the fresh herbs, extra virgin olive oil, red wine vinegar and feta cheese. Serve warm or at room temperature.

Lentils with Eggplant and Greek Yogurt

Serves	Prep	Cooking Time	Release Method
6	**Easier**	**HIGH 8 Minutes**	**Quick**

1 tablespoon olive oil

1 onion, finely chopped

1 medium eggplant, cut into 1-inch cubes

1 (14 ounce) can chopped tomatoes

2 cups French green lentils

2 cups vegetable stock or water

1 teaspoon salt

freshly ground black pepper

¼ cup chopped fresh parsley

¼ cup chopped fresh mint

juice of half a lemon

1 cup Greek yogurt

1. Pre-heat the pressure cooker using the BROWN setting.

2. Add the olive oil and cook the onion for a few minutes. Add the eggplant and tomatoes and stir to coat well. Add the lentils and the stock or water. Season with salt and freshly ground black pepper and lock the lid in place.

3. Pressure cook for 8 minutes on HIGH.

4. Reduce the pressure with the QUICK-RELEASE method and carefully remove the lid.

5. Season to taste with salt and pepper again and stir in the parsley and mint. Squeeze the lemon juice on the lentils and serve with a dollop of Greek yogurt and more freshly ground black pepper.

Farrotto with Asparagus and Lemon

It is believed that farro is the world's most ancient grain – the grain from which all other grains are derived. As a whole grain, it is nutritious and yet delicious too! A farrotto is a risotto with farro in place of the rice.

Serves	Prep	Cooking Time	Release Method
4 to 6	**Easiest**	**HIGH 16 Minutes**	**Quick**

1 tablespoon butter

½ onion, finely chopped

2 cups farro

½ cup white wine

5½ cups chicken stock, vegetable stock or water

1 bunch thinly sliced asparagus, (⅛-inch slices)

zest and juice of 1 lemon

1 teaspoon salt

freshly ground black pepper

½ cup grated Parmesan cheese, plus more for serving

1. Pre-heat the pressure cooker using the BROWN setting.

2. Add the butter and cook the onion until tender. Add the farro and stir to coat well. Add the wine and let the wine simmer with the farro for a few minutes until it has almost disappeared. Add the stock and lock the lid in place.

3. Pressure cook on HIGH for 16 minutes.

4. Reduce the pressure using the QUICK-RELEASE method, and carefully remove the lid.

5. Stir in the thinly sliced asparagus, lemon zest, lemon juice, salt and pepper. Return the lid to the cooker for 3 minutes.

6. Stir in the Parmesan cheese. There will be excess liquid in the pot at this point, but as the farrotto sits for a few minutes, it will absorb the liquid and thicken slightly.

Farrotto with Wild Mushrooms and Chives

The nutty flavor of the farro is perfect for this dish, finished with Parmesan cheese. Use the best, most interesting mushrooms you can find for this dish and you won't be sorry. This is a dish I keep coming back to for more!

Serves	Prep	Cooking Time	Release Method
4 to 6	**Easiest**	**HIGH 18 Minutes**	**Quick**

1 tablespoon butter

½ onion, finely chopped

2 cups wild mushrooms, sliced (shiitake, crimini, porcini, chanterelles, portobellos or any combination)

2 cups farro

½ cup white wine

5½ cups chicken stock, mushroom stock, vegetable stock or water

½ cup chopped fresh chives

½ cup grated Parmesan cheese

1 teaspoon salt

freshly ground black pepper

1. Pre-heat the pressure cooker using the BROWN setting.

2. Add the butter to the cooker and cook the onion for a few minutes. Add the mushrooms and farro and stir to coat well. Add the wine and let the wine simmer with the farro for a few minutes until it has almost disappeared. Pour in the stock, stir once and lock the lid in place.

3. Pressure cook for 18 minutes on HIGH.

4. Reduce the pressure with the QUICK-RELEASE method and carefully remove the lid.

5. Stir in the chives and Parmesan cheese and season the farrotto to taste with salt and freshly ground black pepper. There will be excess liquid in the pot at this point, but as the farrotto sits for a few minutes, it will absorb the liquid and thicken slightly.

Black Beans with Chorizo Sausage

Serves	Prep	Cooking Time	Release Method
4 to 6	**Easier**	**HIGH 5 + 15 Minutes**	**Natural**

3 cups dried black beans

1 tablespoon vegetable oil

1 pound chorizo sausage, casings removed and broken into chunks

2 cloves garlic, minced

1 bay leaf

1 teaspoon salt

1 quart chicken stock

salt and freshly ground black pepper

½ cup chopped fresh cilantro

1. Place the black beans in the pressure cooker and cover with an inch of water. Pressure cook on HIGH for 5 minutes. Let the pressure drop NATURALLY and carefully remove the lid. Drain and set the beans aside.

2. Pre-heat the pressure cooker using the BROWN setting.

3. Add the oil and brown the chorizo sausage. Add the garlic and cook for one more minute. Return the beans to the cooker and add the bay leaf, salt and chicken stock.

4. Pressure cook on HIGH for 15 minutes.

5. Let the pressure drop NATURALLY and carefully remove the lid.

6. Season to taste with salt and pepper and stir in the fresh cilantro.

Baked Beans

These are NOT the same beans that you had out of a can as a kid! Though reminiscent of the canned version, making the beans from scratch results in beans that have a firmer texture and a sauce that is delicious and hard to resist.

Serves	Prep	Cooking Time	Release Method
6 to 8	**Easier**	**HIGH 5 + 18 Minutes**	**Natural**

2 cups dried navy or white beans

½ pound bacon, chopped

1 onion, finely chopped

2 cloves garlic, minced

¼ cup molasses

¼ cup tomato paste

¼ cup brown sugar

2 tablespoons cider vinegar

1 teaspoon dry mustard powder

1 bay leaf

1 teaspoon salt

1. Place the navy beans in the pressure cooker and cover with an inch of water. Pressure cook on HIGH for 5 minutes. Let the pressure drop NATURALLY and carefully remove the lid. Drain and set the beans aside.

2. Pre-heat the pressure cooker using the BROWN setting.

3. Add the bacon and cook until almost crispy. Remove bacon pieces and set aside. Drain off all but 1 tablespoon of the bacon fat. Add the onion and garlic to the cooker and cook for 2 to 3 minutes. Add the remaining ingredients, stir well and return the beans to the cooker. Pour in enough water to just cover the beans (about 2 cups) and lock the lid in place.

4. Pressure cook on HIGH for 18 minutes.

5. Let the pressure drop NATURALLY and carefully remove the lid.

6. Season to taste again with salt and let the beans cool before serving with the reserved cooked bacon sprinkled on top. The beans will continue to absorb liquid and get thicker as they cool.

TIP For a thicker consistency, remove a cup or two of the beans, purée them in a blender or food processor and stir them back into the beans.

White Beans with Pancetta and Kale

Serves	Prep	Cooking Time	Release Method
6 to 8	**Easier**	**HIGH 5 + 15 Minutes**	**Natural**

2 cups dried white beans

8 slices pancetta (or 6 slices bacon), sliced into 1-inch pieces

2 cloves garlic, minced

1 bay leaf

1 teaspoon salt

1 quart chicken stock

salt and freshly ground black pepper

4 cups packed shredded kale

¼ cup grated Parmesan cheese

1. Place the white beans in the pressure cooker and cover with an inch of water. Pressure cook on HIGH for 5 minutes. Let the pressure drop NATURALLY and carefully remove the lid. Drain and set the beans aside.

2. Pre-heat the pressure cooker using the BROWN setting.

3. Add the pancetta and cook until almost crispy. Remove the pancetta from the cooker and set aside. Add the garlic to the cooker and cook for 30 seconds. Return the beans to the cooker and add the bay leaf, salt and chicken stock. Lock the lid in place.

4. Pressure cook on HIGH for 15 minutes.

5. Let the pressure drop NATURALLY and carefully remove the lid.

6. Season to taste with salt and pepper and stir in the kale. Bring the liquid to a simmer using the BROWN setting. Simmer for about 4 to 5 minutes or until the kale is tender and cooked. Stir the cooked pancetta back into the beans and transfer to a serving dish. Sprinkle with Parmesan cheese and serve.

TIP If you can't find, or don't have any kale, substitute spinach and cook for just a minute before returning the pancetta and serving.

Vegetables

Vegetable Cooking Chart

Vegetables are a quick fix in the pressure cooker. They really just take a matter of minutes. To ensure even cooking, cut all the vegetables into uniform shapes and sizes. Some vegetables are better steamed, while others can be fully submerged in whatever cooking liquid you choose. To steam vegetables, use either a steamer basket or a rack that elevates the vegetables above the cooking liquid. The quick-release method is used for vegetables to prevent them from over-cooking.

	Cooking Time at HIGH Pressure	Liquid Needed	Cooking Method	Release Method
Acorn squash halved	8 minutes	1 cup	Steam	Quick
Artichokes medium, whole	12 minutes	1 cup	Steam	Quick
Beets medium	15 minutes	1 cup	Steam	Quick
Broccoli rabe	3 minutes	1 cup	Steam	Quick
Brussels sprouts	4 to 6 minutes	1 cup	Steam	Quick
Butternut squash 1-inch chunks	5 minutes	1 cup	Submerged	Quick
Cabbage, red or green quartered	4 to 6 minutes	1 cup	Submerged	Quick
Cauliflower whole	5 minutes	1 cup	Steam	Quick
Carrots ½-inch slices	4 minutes	1 cup	Submerged	Quick
Collard greens	5 to 10 minutes	1 cup	Submerged	Quick
Corn on the cob	2 to 3 minutes	1 cup	Steam	Quick
Eggplant	3 to 4 minutes	1 cup	Submerged	Quick
Fennel wedges	4 minutes	1 cup	Submerged	Quick
Kale	4 minutes	1 cup	Submerged	Quick
Leeks 1-inch pieces	4 minutes	1 cup	Submerged	Quick
Parsnips	5 minutes	1 cup	Steam	Quick
Potatoes small whole	6 to 7 minutes	1 cup	Submerged	Quick
Potatoes 1-inch chunks	8 to 10 minutes	1 cup	Submerged	Quick
Rutabaga 1-inch chunks	4 minutes	1 cup	Submerged	Quick
Spaghetti squash halved	12 to 15 minutes	1 cup	Steam	Quick
Sweet potatoes 1-inch chunks	5 minutes	1 cup	Submerged	Quick
Swiss chard	2 minutes	1 cup	Submerged	Quick

Broccoli Rabe with Italian Sausage

I like the spiciness that the hot Italian sausage gives to the broccoli rabe, but the nice thing about this recipe is that you can customize and use pork sausage, turkey sausage or chicken sausage. You can even make this a vegetarian dish by using no sausage at all and vegetable stock instead of chicken stock.

Serves	Prep	Cooking Time	Release Method
4 to 6	**Easiest**	**HIGH 3 Minutes**	**Quick**

1 tablespoon olive oil

2 links Italian sausage (hot or sweet), casings removed and broken into chunks

2 heads broccoli rabe, stems trimmed

1½ cups chicken stock

salt and freshly ground black pepper

1. Pre-heat the pressure cooker using the BROWN setting.

2. Add the oil and cook the sausage until nicely browned. Add the broccoli rabe. The pressure cooker will be very full, but the broccoli rabe will reduce in volume significantly. Add the stock, season with salt and freshly ground black pepper and lock the lid in place.

3. Pressure cook on HIGH for 3 minutes.

4. Release the pressure with the QUICK-RELEASE method and carefully remove the lid. Transfer the broccoli rabe and sausage to a serving plate with a slotted spoon, season to taste with salt and freshly ground black pepper and moisten with only as much liquid as you would like.

Spicy Fennel with Pinenuts and Currants

Fennel has a slightly sweet licorice flavor and a nice crunch to it. I love raw fennel sliced into salads, but I also love fennel braised. In this recipe it is tossed with pinenuts and currants. This would be a delicious side dish to a roast chicken.

Serves	Prep	Cooking Time	Release Method
6	**Easiest**	**HIGH 4 Minutes**	**Quick**

2 tablespoons olive oil

1 onion, chopped

1 clove garlic, minced

¼ teaspoon crushed red pepper flakes

2 bulbs fennel, cut into wedges

½ cup dried currants

1½ cups vegetable stock

½ teaspoon salt

freshly ground black pepper

¼ cup toasted pinenuts

¼ cup chopped fresh parsley

1. Pre-heat the pressure cooker using the BROWN setting.

2. Add the oil and cook the onion, garlic and pepper flakes for a minute or two. Add the fennel wedges and currants and stir to coat everything with oil. Add the stock, season with salt and freshly ground black pepper and lock the lid in place.

3. Pressure cook on HIGH for 4 minutes.

4. Release the pressure with the QUICK-RELEASE method and carefully remove the lid.

5. Transfer the fennel to a serving plate with a slotted spoon, season to taste with salt and freshly ground black pepper and scatter the toasted pinenuts and parsley over the top.

TIP To prepare fennel, cut off the long stalks, leaving just the bulb. Remove any tough or fibrous outer leaves from the bulb and chop or slice the bulb into the desired shape. The core at the base of the bulb will help hold the wedges together, but if you are slicing fennel into salads, remove the tough core and discard.

Pumpkin Pie Spiced Sweet Potatoes

Serves	Prep	Cooking Time	Release Method
6 to 8	**Easiest**	**HIGH 5 Minutes**	**Quick**

6 to 8 large sweet potatoes, peeled and cut into 1-inch chunks (about 10 cups)

3 tablespoons butter, melted

½ teaspoon ground cinnamon

½ teaspoon ground nutmeg

¼ teaspoon ground ginger

¼ teaspoon ground allspice

pinch ground cloves

1 teaspoon salt

freshly ground black pepper

chopped fresh chives for garnish

1. Place the potatoes into the pressure cooker and add enough water to just cover the vegetables. Lock the lid in place.

2. Pressure cook on HIGH for 5 minutes.

3. Reduce the pressure with the QUICK-RELEASE method and carefully remove the lid.

4. Drain the potatoes and return them to the warm pressure cooker. Add the butter and spices and mash the potatoes with a potato masher or pass through a food mill. Season to taste with salt and freshly ground black pepper and garnish with chopped fresh chives.

TIP You can substitute store-bought pumpkin pie spice for the spices in this recipe.

Parsnip and Sweet Potato Mash with Brown Butter

While you don't have to brown the butter for this recipe, it adds such a delicious nuttiness to the vegetables. It doesn't take long and you've got five minutes to kill while the vegetables cook!

Serves	Prep	Cooking Time	Release Method
6	**Easiest**	**HIGH 5 Minutes**	**Quick**

2 pounds parsnips, peeled and sliced

2 pounds sweet potatoes, peeled and cut into chunks

¼ cup butter

1 tablespoon chopped fresh thyme

salt and freshly ground black pepper

1. Place the parsnips and sweet potato into the pressure cooker and add 2 cups of water. Lock the lid in place.

2. Pressure cook on HIGH for 5 minutes. While the vegetables are cooking, heat the butter in a small saucepan on the stovetop over medium heat. Let the butter cook until it turns light brown in color and smells nutty. You will see browned solids on the bottom of the pan.

3. Reduce the pressure using the QUICK-RELEASE method and carefully remove the lid.

4. Drain the vegetables and transfer them to a bowl. Mash the parsnips and sweet potatoes together with the brown butter and thyme using either a masher or a food mill or a good wooden spoon. Season to taste with salt and freshly ground black pepper.

TIP Peeled parsnips will turn dark when exposed to the air for a period of time. To avoid this, either use the parsnips right away, or leave them in a bowl of water with half a squeezed lemon.

Sweet Potato and Apple Mash

Serves	Prep	Cooking Time	Release Method
6	**Easiest**	**HIGH 5 Minutes**	**Quick**

3 pounds sweet potatoes, peeled and cut into 1-inch chunks

2 Granny Smith apples, peeled, cored and chopped

3 tablespoons butter, melted

salt and freshly ground black pepper

5 scallions, sliced (optional)

1. Place the potatoes and apples into the pressure cooker and add enough water to just cover the vegetables. Lock the lid in place.

2. Pressure cook on HIGH for 5 minutes.

3. Reduce the pressure with the QUICK-RELEASE method and carefully remove the lid.

4. Drain the potatoes and return them to the warm pressure cooker. Add the butter and mash the potatoes and apples using a potato masher, a food mill or a good wooden spoon. Season to taste with salt and freshly ground black pepper and garnish with scallions.

TIP

Choose sweet potatoes that are not wrinkled and have no blemishes. Store them in a cool place, but not the refrigerator. In the refrigerator, they can develop a hard core and strange taste.

Collard Greens with Smoked Ham

Serves	Prep	Cooking Time	Release Method
6	**Easiest**	**HIGH 10 Minutes**	**Quick**

1 tablespoon oil

1 onion, sliced

2 cloves garlic, smashed

¼ teaspoon crushed red pepper flakes

1 ham hock

2 cups chicken stock

2 bunches collard greens, stemmed and cut into 1-inch pieces (about 15 cups)

1 cup finely diced smoked ham

salt and freshly ground black pepper

1. Pre-heat the pressure cooker using the BROWN setting.

2. Add the oil and cook the onion, garlic and red pepper flakes for a minute or two. Add the ham hock and the chicken stock. Stir in the collard greens and lock the lid in place.

3. Pressure cook on HIGH for 10 minutes.

4. Reduce the pressure using the QUICK-RELEASE method and carefully remove the lid.

5. Remove the ham hock from the cooker and stir in the diced smoked ham. Season to taste with salt and pepper (you shouldn't need much, if any salt). Transfer the collard greens to a serving dish with a slotted spoon.

Spaghetti Squash
with Parmesan-Parsley and Breadcrumbs

There are not a lot of ingredients in this recipe, so it's really important that you use the best ingredients you can. Try to get true Parmigiano-Reggiano cheese and make your own breadcrumbs if you can.

Serves	Prep	Cooking Time	Release Method
4 to 6	**Easiest**	**HIGH 12 to 15 Minutes**	**Quick**

1 spaghetti squash, halved and seeds removed

salt and freshly ground black pepper

2 cups toasted coarse breadcrumbs

½ cup grated Parmesan cheese

¼ cup chopped fresh parsley

extra virgin olive oil

1. Season the cut side of the spaghetti squash with salt and pepper. Place the spaghetti squash halves, cut side down on a rack in the pressure cooker (it's ok if they rest on top of each other). Add 2 cups of water to the cooker and lock the lid in place.

2. Pressure cook on HIGH for 12 to 15 minutes (depending on the size of the spaghetti squash). While the squash is cooking, combine the toasted breadcrumbs, Parmesan cheese and parsley. Season the crumb mixture to taste with salt and freshly ground black pepper.

3. Reduce the pressure with the QUICK-RELEASE method and carefully remove the lid.

4. Remove the spaghetti squash halves from the cooker using tongs. When the squash is cool enough to handle, scrape the flesh of the squash with a fork, pulling the strands of squash away from the skin. Toss the spaghetti squash with the breadcrumbs, drizzle with a little extra virgin olive oil and serve.

TIP To make your own coarse breadcrumbs, pulse fresh Italian bread or baguette in a food processor until the crumbs are the desired size. Toast them on a baking sheet in a 350º F oven for 10 to 15 minutes or until they are crunchy.

Corn on the Cob
with Sun-Dried Tomato and Basil Butter

Corn cooks very quickly in the pressure cooker and because it is steamed rather than boiled, it retains more of its nutrients this way. If you are using corn at peak season, it will only need 2 minutes of cooking time. If the corn is out of season, however, it will probably need another minute in the cooker.

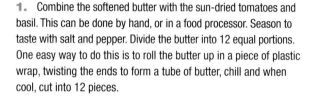

Serves	Prep	Cooking Time	Release Method
6	**Easier**	**HIGH 2-3 Minutes**	**Quick**

½ cup butter, softened

3 tablespoons chopped sun-dried tomatoes

3 tablespoons chopped fresh basil

salt and freshly ground black pepper

6 cobs of corn

1. Combine the softened butter with the sun-dried tomatoes and basil. This can be done by hand, or in a food processor. Season to taste with salt and pepper. Divide the butter into 12 equal portions. One easy way to do this is to roll the butter up in a piece of plastic wrap, twisting the ends to form a tube of butter, chill and when cool, cut into 12 pieces.

2. Place a rack or steamer basket into the pressure cooker. Add two cups of water to the cooker. Wrap each cob of corn with two pieces of the butter in aluminum foil, and place on the rack or steamer basket.

3. Pressure cook on HIGH for 2 to 3 minutes.

4. Reduce the pressure using the QUICK-RELEASE method and carefully remove the lid.

5. Unwrap the cobs of corn and serve, pouring the extra melted butter over the top and seasoning again with salt and freshly ground black pepper.

TIP If you're making this compound butter, why not double the recipe and freeze what you have left over. It is delicious on grilled chicken or steak!

Braised Cabbage with Prosciutto and Cream

This recipe is delicious and is a favorite of mine! It feels like a comfort food side dish that is bound to warm you up on a winter night.

Serves	Prep	Cooking Time	Release Method
8 to 10	**Easier**	**HIGH 6 Minutes**	**Quick**

2 tablespoons butter

1 white onion, sliced

1 small head Savoy cabbage, cored and cut into 1-inch slices

1 cup chicken stock

2 cups heavy cream

1½ teaspoons salt

freshly ground black pepper

8 thin slices prosciutto, sliced into strips

¼ cup chopped fresh parsley

1. Pre-heat the pressure cooker using the BROWN setting.

2. Add the butter and cook the onion for a few minutes. Add the cabbage to the cooker and stir well to coat. Cook for a minute or two. Combine the chicken stock, cream, salt and pepper and pour it over the top of the cabbage. Lock the lid in place.

3. Pressure cook on HIGH for 6 minutes.

4. Reduce the pressure using the QUICK-RELEASE method and carefully remove the lid.

5. Transfer the cabbage to a serving dish and toss with the prosciutto and parsley.

 Savoy cabbage is the prettiest of cabbages with loose, dark green crinkly leaves on the outside and pale green leaves on the inside. It is tender and sweet and doesn't have the sulfurous odor of other cabbages.

Carrots with Orange and Rosemary

Since the carrots in this recipe are the main star, rather than the supporting cast, buy the nicest looking carrots you can.

Serves	Prep	Cooking Time	Release Method
6	**Easier**	**HIGH 4 Minutes**	**Quick**

2 tablespoons butter

1 shallot, finely chopped

6 large carrots, peeled and sliced on the bias (½-inch slices)

1 tablespoon honey

1 tablespoon chopped fresh rosemary

1½ cups orange juice

salt and freshly ground black pepper

1. Pre-heat the pressure cooker using the BROWN setting.

2. Add the butter and cook the shallot for a minute or two. Add the carrots and stir to coat well with the butter. Add the remaining ingredients and lock the lid in place.

3. Pressure cook on HIGH for 4 minutes.

4. Reduce the pressure using the QUICK-RELEASE method and carefully remove the lid.

5. Transfer the carrots to a serving dish with a slotted spoon. If desired, simmer the liquid in the pressure cooker using the BROWN setting until it has reduced to the desired consistency and pour over the carrots. Garnish with a sprig of fresh rosemary.

TIP When buying carrots for this dish, choose carrots with bright green tops still attached. Remove the tops as soon as you get home, since they will continue to live off the nutrients in the carrots, and it's better to have all the nutrients remain in the carrots.

Buttery Braised Leeks

Serves	Prep	Cooking Time	Release Method
6	**Easiest**	**HIGH 4 Minutes**	**Quick**

4 tablespoons butter, divided

5 leeks, dark green leaves removed, cleaned and chopped into 1-inch pieces (about 12 cups)

½ cup white wine

1 cup chicken stock

salt and freshly ground black pepper

grated Parmesan cheese (optional)

1. Pre-heat the pressure cooker using the BROWN setting.

2. Add 2 tablespoons of the butter and cook the leeks for a minute or two. Add the white wine and bring to a simmer. Add the chicken stock and lock the lid in place.

3. Pressure cook on HIGH for 4 minutes.

4. Reduce the pressure using the QUICK-RELEASE method and carefully remove the lid.

5. Season to taste with salt and pepper and stir in the remaining butter. Serve with grated Parmesan cheese.

TIP

To clean leeks, cut off the dark green top of the leek where it naturally wants to break if you bend the leek from end to end. Then, slice the leek in half lengthwise and soak in cold water for 10 minutes or so, separating the leaves with your hands to remove any embedded dirt there. Dry the leeks on a clean kitchen towel and proceed with the recipe.

Brussels Sprouts with Bacon and Parmesan

Though Brussels sprouts may be one of the least popular vegetables in America, they might be hard to pass up with bacon and Parmesan cheese mixed in!

Serves	Prep	Cooking Time	Release Method
6	**Easiest**	**HIGH 6 Minutes**	**Quick**

5 slices bacon, chopped

1 pound Brussels sprouts, trimmed and halved

¼ cup shaved Parmesan cheese

1. Pre-heat the pressure cooker using the BROWN setting.

2. Add the bacon and cook until crispy. Remove the bacon to a side dish and set aside. Wipe out the pressure cooker.

3. Place the Brussels sprouts into a steamer basket and lower the steamer basket into the pressure cooker. Add 2 cups of water to the cooker and lock the lid in place.

4. Pressure cook on HIGH for 6 minutes.

5. Reduce the pressure using the QUICK-RELEASE method and carefully open the lid.

6. Remove the Brussels sprouts and toss with the crispy bacon pieces and the shaved Parmesan cheese before serving.

Ratatouille

There are cooks who argue about the proper way to make ratatouille – cook all the vegetables separately and then mix them together, or cook them all together in a pan. This version follows the latter argument and results in a wetter ratatouille than most, but the flavors are intense.

Serves	Prep	Cooking Time	Release Method
8 to 10	**Easier**	**HIGH 4 Minutes**	**Quick**

2 tablespoons olive oil

1 onion, chopped

1 clove garlic, minced

1 red bell pepper, chopped
(1-inch chunks)

1 yellow bell pepper, chopped
(1-inch chunks)

1 eggplant, cut into large chunks
(1-inch chunks)

2 zucchini, cut into large chunks
(1-inch chunks)

½ teaspoon dried thyme

½ teaspoon dried basil

¼ teaspoon dried rosemary

1 (14 ounce) can crushed tomatoes

1 (14 ounce) can chopped tomatoes

1½ cups water

salt and freshly ground black pepper

Parmesan cheese, shredded

1. Pre-heat the pressure cooker using the BROWN setting.

2. Add the oil and cook the onion, garlic and peppers for a minute or two. Add the eggplant and zucchini, thyme, basil and rosemary and mix well. Add the tomatoes and water, season with salt and freshly ground black pepper and lock the lid in place.

3. Pressure cook on HIGH for 4 minutes.

4. Release the pressure with the QUICK-RELEASE method and carefully remove the lid.

5. Season to taste with salt and freshly ground black pepper and sprinkle the shredded Parmesan cheese on top.

Sweet and Sour Red Cabbage

Serves	Prep	Cooking Time	Release Method
6	**Easier**	**HIGH 5 Minutes**	**Quick**

1 tablespoon vegetable oil

1 red onion, sliced

2 pounds red cabbage, sliced (about 12 cups)

2 Granny Smith apples, peeled, cored and chopped

½ cup brown sugar

2 teaspoons caraway seeds

½ cup apple cider vinegar

½ cup balsamic vinegar

1 cup apple juice

salt and freshly ground black pepper

1. Pre-heat the pressure cooker using the BROWN setting.

2. Add the oil and cook the onion for a minute or two. Add the cabbage and apple and stir well. Combine the brown sugar, caraway seeds, apple cider vinegar, balsamic vinegar and apple juice, stir well and then pour the mixture over the cabbage. Lock the lid in place.

3. Pressure cook on HIGH for 5 minutes.

4. Reduce the pressure using the QUICK-RELEASE method and carefully remove the lid.

5. Season to taste with salt and pepper and transfer to a serving dish.

Steamed Artichokes with Lemon Aïoli

Artichokes come in many different sizes. When choosing artichokes for this recipe, make sure whatever you buy will fit into your pressure cooker. Artichokes are fun to eat as you pull off each leaf, dip it in the aïoli and draw the base of the leaf through your teeth to scrape off the soft part of the leaf. Remember to put out a bowl for the discarded leaves.

Serves	Prep	Cooking Time	Release Method
4 to 6	**Easier**	**HIGH 12 Minutes**	**Quick**

1 cup mayonnaise

1 large clove garlic, minced and mashed into a paste

1 tablespoon lemon zest

2 tablespoons lemon juice

1 tablespoon chopped fresh chives

salt and freshly ground black pepper

4 medium artichokes

1 lemon

4 or 5 sprigs fresh thyme

1. Make the aioli by mixing together the mayonnaise, mashed garlic, lemon zest and juice, chives, salt and pepper in a bowl.

2. Prepare the artichokes by cutting off the top inch of the prickly leaves, or if you're not bothered by the prickly leaves, leave the artichokes whole. Cut off the stem to create a flat base.

3. Place a rack in the pressure cooker and rest the artichokes on top of the rack. Squeeze the lemon juice all over the artichokes and drop the squeezed halves into the cooker around the artichokes along with the fresh thyme sprigs. Add 2 cups of water to the cooker and lock the lid in place.

4. Pressure cook on HIGH for 12 minutes.

5. Reduce the pressure using the QUICK-RELEASE method and carefully remove the lid.

6. Before you transfer the artichokes to a serving dish, invert them over the pressure cooker to allow any hot water to escape from between the leaves. Serve with the aioli.

TIP Peak season for artichokes is from March to May. Squeeze the artichoke together when selecting – the leaves should squeak if it's ripe.

Beets with Tarragon and Orange Balsamic

Beets usually take up to 45 minutes in the oven to roast. In the pressure cooker, that time is reduced to 15 minutes! You can choose to peel the beets with a peeler before steaming if you like, but the peel comes off very easily with a paring knife once they are steamed.

Serves	Prep	Cooking Time	Release Method
4 to 6	**Easiest**	**HIGH 15 Minutes**	**Quick**

4 large beets, scrubbed

1¾ cups orange juice, divided

2 tablespoons balsamic vinegar

2 tablespoons olive oil

salt and freshly ground black pepper

1 tablespoon chopped fresh tarragon

1. Place the beets into a steamer basket and place the steamer basket on a rack in the pressure cooker. Add 1½ cups of the orange juice to the cooker and lock the lid in place.

2. Pressure cook on HIGH for 15 minutes. While the beets are cooking, make the dressing. Combine the remaining ¼ cup of the orange juice with the balsamic vinegar, olive oil, salt and pepper.

3. Reduce the pressure with the QUICK-RELEASE method and carefully remove the lid.

4. Let the beets sit until they are cool enough to handle. Peel the beets and cut them into wedges or thick slices. Toss the beets with the dressing and the fresh tarragon and serve warm or at room temperature.

Potatoes Boulangère

Boulangère potatoes are similar to, but lighter than au gratin potatoes in that they are cooked in stock rather than cream. These potatoes don't get the browning that oven-baked potatoes Boulangère would have, but you can finish them in the oven afterwards if you like.

Serves	Prep	Cooking Time	Release Method
8	**Easier**	**HIGH 15 Minutes**	**Natural**

8 slices bacon, chopped

1 white onion, sliced

1 clove garlic, minced

1 tablespoon fresh thyme leaves

6 large Russet potatoes, peeled and cut into wedges lengthwise

1½ cups chicken stock

1 teaspoon salt

freshly ground black pepper

½ lemon

1. Pre-heat the pressure cooker using the BROWN setting.

2. Add the bacon to the cooker and cook until the bacon is crispy. Remove the bacon from the cooker with a slotted spoon and set aside. Add the onion and garlic and cook for several minutes, until the onion starts to brown. Add the thyme and potatoes to the onions and stir to mix well. Add the stock, salt and pepper and lock the lid in place.

3. Pressure cook on HIGH for 15 minutes.

4. Let the pressure drop NATURALLY and carefully remove the lid.

5. Let the potatoes cool a little before spooning out portions from the pressure cooker. Squeeze the lemon half over the potatoes and garnish with the reserved bacon.

TIP For a decadent side dish, spoon some of these potatoes into a dish, top with Parmesan cheese, and heat under the broiler for a minute or two, or until the cheese browns.

Pasta
and
Sauces

Arrabbiata Sauce

Arrabbiata sauce comes from the Italian word for angry, referring to the spicy chili flake in this simple but delicious tomato pasta sauce with bacon.

Serves	Prep	Cooking Time	Release Method
6 to 8	**Easiest**	**HIGH 5 Minutes**	**Quick**

12 slices of bacon, chopped

2 cloves garlic, finely chopped

½ teaspoon crushed red pepper flakes

2 (28 ounce) cans diced tomatoes

1 teaspoon salt

freshly ground black pepper

¼ cup chopped fresh parsley

grated Parmesan cheese (optional)

1. Pre-heat the pressure cooker using the BROWN setting.

2. Add the bacon and cook until almost crispy. Remove the bacon with a slotted spoon and set aside. Add the garlic and red pepper flakes for a minute or two. Add the tomatoes, salt and pepper and lock the lid in place.

3. Pressure cook on HIGH for 5 minutes.

4. Reduce the pressure using the QUICK-RELEASE method and carefully remove the lid.

5. Return the cooked bacon to the cooker and season to taste with salt and freshly ground black pepper. Stir in parsley and serve over pasta with grated Parmesan cheese.

Tomato Vodka Sauce

Serves	Prep	Cooking Time	Release Method
6 to 8	**Easiest**	**HIGH 8 Minutes**	**Quick**

2 tablespoons olive oil

2 cloves garlic, minced

½ teaspoon crushed red pepper flakes

1 cup vodka

2 (28 ounce) cans of diced tomatoes OR 6 cups chopped fresh tomatoes

1 cup heavy cream

1 teaspoon salt

freshly ground black pepper

¼ cup chopped fresh parsley or basil

grated Parmesan cheese (optional)

1. Pre-heat the pressure cooker using the BROWN setting.

2. Add the olive oil and cook the garlic and crushed red pepper flakes briefly until the garlic is fragrant, but do not brown. Pour in the vodka and let it simmer for a minute or two, until it has reduced by at least half. Add the tomatoes, cream, salt and pepper and lock the lid in place.

3. Pressure cook on HIGH for 8 minutes.

4. Reduce the pressure with the QUICK-RELEASE method, and carefully remove the lid.

5. Season to taste with salt and freshly ground black pepper and stir in parsley or basil. Serve over pasta and sprinkle with grated Parmesan cheese.

 TIP Make sure you bring the vodka to a simmer in this recipe. That will allow the alcohol to boil off and evaporate.

Quick and Easy Mac 'n' Cheese

This is the easiest Mac 'n' Cheese ever!

Serves	Prep	Cooking Time	Release Method
4 to 6	**Easiest**	**HIGH 6 Minutes**	**Quick**

1 tablespoon olive oil

1 pound macaroni

2½ cups water

½ cup heavy cream

1½ cups grated Cheddar cheese

½ cup grated Parmesan cheese

2 ounces cream cheese

salt and freshly ground pepper

¼ cup fresh parsley, chopped

1. Pre-heat the pressure cooker using the BROWN setting.

2. Add the oil and stir in the dry macaroni to coat. Pour in the water and lock the lid in place.

3. Pressure cook on HIGH for 6 minutes.

4. Reduce the pressure with QUICK-RELEASE method and carefully remove the lid.

5. Immediately add all remaining ingredients and stir well. Season to taste with salt and pepper and garnish with freshly chopped parsley.

TIP It's easy to mix things up with this recipe for Mac 'n' Cheese by just adding cooked ingredients at the end. Try stirring in cooked bacon, cherry tomatoes, caramelized onion or any combination of ingredients.

Tomato Sauce with Capers and Kalamata Olives

Here's a little Mediterranean twist to a marinara sauce for pasta. This is also great served with the Greek Meatballs on page 116.

Serves	Prep	Cooking Time	Release Method
6 to 8	**Easiest**	**HIGH 5 Minutes**	**Quick**

1 tablespoon olive oil

1 onion, finely chopped

2 cloves garlic, minced

¼ teaspoon crushed red pepper flakes

1 (28 ounce) can of crushed tomatoes

1 (28 ounce) can of diced tomatoes

1 (12 ounce) jar of roasted red peppers, drained and chopped

¾ cup Kalamata olives, sliced or halved, pits removed

3 tablespoons capers

2 tablespoons balsamic vinegar

freshly ground black pepper

¼ cup chopped fresh parsley

grated Parmesan or crumbled feta cheese (optional)

1. Pre-heat the pressure cooker using the BROWN setting.

2. Add the olive oil and cook the onion, garlic and crushed red pepper flakes for a minute or two. Add the tomatoes, roasted red peppers, olives, capers, balsamic vinegar and lock the lid in place.

3. Pressure cook on HIGH for 5 minutes.

4. Reduce the pressure using the QUICK-RELEASE method and carefully remove the lid.

5. Season to taste with freshly ground black pepper. Stir in parsley and serve over pasta with grated Parmesan cheese or crumbled feta cheese.

Penne with Butternut Squash and Broccoli Rabe

Serves	Prep	Cooking Time	Release Method
6	**Easier**	**HIGH 6 Minutes**	**Quick**

1 tablespoon olive oil

½ onion, finely chopped

1 clove garlic, minced

pinch crushed red pepper flakes

3 cups chopped butternut squash
(1-inch cubes)

1 bunch broccoli rabe, stems trimmed
and cut into 1-inch pieces

12 ounces dried penne

3 cups chicken or vegetable stock

½ teaspoon salt

freshly ground black pepper

grated Parmesan cheese (optional)

1. Pre-heat the pressure cooker using the BROWN setting.

2. Add the olive oil and cook the onion, garlic and pepper flakes for a minute or two. Add the butternut squash and broccoli rabe and continue to cook for 2 to 3 minutes. Stir in the pasta, stock and salt, and lock the lid in place.

3. Pressure cook on HIGH for 6 minutes.

4. Reduce the pressure with the QUICK-RELEASE method and carefully remove the lid.

5. There should still be some broth left in the pot with which to moisten this pasta dish. Season to taste with salt and freshly ground black pepper and serve with grated Parmesan cheese.

TIP

Broccoli rabe, also known as rapini, is not actually related to broccoli, but is a member of the turnip family.

Cheesy Macaroni and Sweet Italian Sausage

The ketchup in this recipe gives a sweet note to the pasta that will keep you coming back for more. It's a terrific one dish meal that the whole family will enjoy.

Serves	Prep	Cooking Time	Release Method
6	**Easier**	**HIGH 6 Minutes**	**Quick**

1 tablespoon vegetable oil

1 pound sweet Italian sausage, casings removed and broken into chunks

1 onion, finely chopped

1 yellow bell pepper, chopped

1 red bell pepper, chopped

1½ teaspoons dried oregano

1½ teaspoons dried basil

1 teaspoon paprika

1 teaspoon salt

freshly ground black pepper

1 (28 ounce) can diced tomatoes

1 cup beef stock

¼ cup ketchup

12 ounces dried elbow macaroni

grated Parmesan cheese OR
1½ cups grated Cheddar cheese

1. Pre-heat the pressure cooker using the BROWN setting.

2. Add the oil to the cooker and brown the sausage. Add the onion, peppers, herbs and spices, salt and pepper and continue to cook for a few minutes, stirring well. Add the tomatoes, stock, ketchup and elbow macaroni and lock the lid in place.

3. Pressure cook on HIGH for 6 minutes.

4. Reduce the pressure with the QUICK-RELEASE method and carefully remove the lid.

5. Give the ingredients a good stir, season to taste with salt and pepper, and serve with grated Parmesan cheese or for a cheesier dish, stir in the grated Cheddar cheese. Let everything rest for a few minutes before serving.

Rigatoni with Italian Sausage, Sun-Dried Tomatoes and Artichokes

This might be one of my all-time favorite pasta sauces. Here, the pasta cooks right in with the sauce, soaking up all the delicious flavors.

Serves	Prep	Cooking Time	Release Method
4 to 6	**Easier**	**HIGH 7 Minutes**	**Quick**

2 pounds hot Italian sausage, casings removed and crumbled (about 4 links)

2 red bell peppers, cut into large chunks

1 yellow bell pepper, cut into large chunks

2 cloves garlic, minced

pinch crushed red pepper flakes

½ cup red wine

2 cups chicken stock

1 (28 ounce) can crushed tomatoes

1 (8.5 ounce) jar sun-dried tomatoes, drained

1 (14 ounce) jar artichokes (marinated or water packed), drained

12 ounces dried rigatoni pasta

salt and freshly ground black pepper

grated Parmesan cheese (optional)

1. Pre-heat the pressure cooker using the BROWN setting.

2. Add the crumbled sausage and cook until browned. Remove the sausage with a slotted spoon and set aside. Add the peppers, garlic and red pepper flakes to the cooker and cook for a few minutes. Add the wine and bring to a simmer. Add the chicken stock, crushed tomatoes, sun-dried tomatoes and artichokes, and return the sausage to the pan. Stir in the rigatoni, pushing it under the liquid and lock the lid in place.

3. Pressure cook on HIGH for 7 minutes.

4. Reduce the pressure using the QUICK-RELEASE method and carefully remove the lid.

5. Season to taste with salt and freshly ground black pepper. Serve with Parmesan cheese.

Sweet Apple Marinara Sauce

This is a light and clean pasta sauce that freezes really well. Why not make a big batch and save some for a rainy day?

Serves	Prep	Cooking Time	Release Method
6 to 8	**Easier**	**HIGH 8 Minutes**	**Quick**

1 tablespoon olive oil

1 onion, finely chopped

2 cloves garlic, minced

2 (28 ounce) cans of diced tomatoes

2 to 3 Granny Smith apples, peeled and grated (about 2 cups)

1 teaspoon salt

freshly ground black pepper

¼ cup chopped fresh parsley

1. Pre-heat the pressure cooker using the BROWN setting. Add the olive oil and cook the onion until tender. Add the garlic and cook for another minute. Add the tomatoes, grated apple, salt and pepper and lock the lid in place.

2. Pressure cook on HIGH for 8 minutes.

3. Reduce the pressure with the QUICK-RELEASE method, and carefully remove the lid.

4. Season to taste with salt and freshly ground black pepper. Stir in parsley and serve over pasta with a drizzle of extra virgin olive oil and a sprinkling of grated Parmesan cheese.

TIP

Instead of coring the apples and then grating them, use the core in the apple to hold on to while you grate the flesh of the fruit.

Tomato Apple Chutney

This chutney pairs beautifully with pork, meat pies, and would even be nice on a burger for a change.

Makes Approximately	Prep	Cooking Time	Release Method
6 Cups	**Easy**	**HIGH 5 Minutes**	**Natural**

1 large red onion, finely chopped

2 cloves garlic, minced

4 apples, peeled, cored and chopped

10 tomatoes, chopped

1 cup golden raisins

1½ cups brown sugar

2 sticks of cinnamon, broken in half

1 teaspoon salt

1 teaspoon crushed red pepper flakes

1½ cups apple cider vinegar

1 tablespoon lemon juice

1. Combine all ingredients in the pressure cooker and lock the lid in place.

2. Pressure cook on HIGH for 5 minutes.

3. Let the pressure drop NATURALLY and carefully remove the lid. This chutney is relatively thin. For a thicker chutney, simmer the sauce in the cooker using the BROWN setting until the desired consistency is reached.

4. Cool the chutney and then store in glass jars in the refrigerator.

Mango Chutney

Mango chutney is nice with all kinds of Indian cuisine, but it is also delicious with just a piece of sharp Cheddar or to spice up some roast chicken.

Makes Approximately	Prep	Cooking Time	Release Method
8 Cups	**Easy**	**HIGH 5 Minutes**	**Natural**

3 apples, peeled, cored and chopped (about 3 cups)

6 to 8 mangoes, peeled and chopped (about 6 cups)

1 cup golden raisins

1 large red onion, finely chopped

2 red bell peppers, finely chopped

¼ cup finely grated fresh gingerroot

1 cup brown sugar

½ cup honey

2 sticks of cinnamon, broken in half

2 tablespoons curry powder

1 teaspoon salt

1 teaspoon brown mustard seeds, whole

1 cup apple cider vinegar

1 cup unsweetened pineapple juice

2 tablespoons lemon juice

1. Combine all ingredients in the pressure cooker and lock the lid in place.

2. Pressure cook on HIGH for 5 minutes.

3. Let the pressure drop NATURALLY and carefully remove the lid.

4. Cool the chutney and then store in glass jars in the refrigerator. Serve with pork, chicken, or turkey, or even as an accompaniment to a Cheddar cheese.

TIP Trying to dice a peeled mango is frustrating – it will slip out of your hands constantly. To dice it easily, slice off the sides of the mango, as closely as possible to the long flat seed inside. Then score each half of the mango flesh into dice, cutting right down to the skin, but not through it. Invert the piece of mango as though you were trying to turn it inside out, and simply cut the dice off the peel.

Desserts

Poached Pears and Peaches

Rum Raisin Rice Pudding

Coconut Rice Pudding with Pineapple

Strawberry Rhubarb Compote with Balsamic Vinegar

Port Cherry Compote

Ginger Peach Compote

Blueberry Cinnamon Compote

Stewed Apples and Plums

Caramel Pot de Crème

Dark Chocolate Orange Pot de Crème

Vanilla Cheesecake

White Chocolate Raspberry Cheesecake

Chocolate Chunk Cheesecake

Bread and Butter Pudding

Annie's Chocolate Hazelnut Banana Bread and Butter Pudding

Marmalade Bread and Butter Pudding

Toffee Apple Bread Pudding

Poached Pears and Peaches

Are you kidding me? One minute of cooking time? That's right – this is a super quick dessert recipe. Served over pound cake, it's a delicious end to a summer meal.

Serves	Prep	Cooking Time	Release Method
6	**Easiest**	**HIGH 1 Minute**	**Quick**

2 cups white wine

1 cinnamon stick

½ - ¾ cup brown sugar

1 vanilla bean, split

3 pears, peeled, cored and cut into quarters

3 peaches, pit removed and halved

1. Combine the wine, cinnamon, sugar and vanilla bean in the pressure cooker and bring to a simmer using the BROWN setting. Stir to dissolve the sugar.

2. Add the pears and peaches and lock the lid in place.

3. Pressure cook on HIGH for 1 minute.

4. Reduce the pressure using the QUICK-RELEASE method and carefully remove the lid.

5. Remove the pears and peaches from the cooker using a slotted spoon and set aside to cool. While the fruit is cooling, reduce the poaching liquid by simmering it using the BROWN setting for about 15 minutes. When the liquid has reached a syrupy consistency, remove, cool and pour as much as you'd like over the poached fruit. Serve over pound cake, ice cream, or cheesecake.

TIP Leaving the peach skins on in this recipe gives the sauce a beautiful color. If you don't like to eat the skin of a peach, it is very easy to peel off after the peaches have cooked and cooled.

Rum Raisin Rice Pudding

This is like a warm version of rum raisin ice cream. Yum!

Serves	Prep	Cooking Time	Release Method
6 to 8	**Easiest**	**HIGH 12 Minutes**	**Quick**

2 cups half and half

2 cups milk

1 tablespoon butter

½ cup sugar

1½ cups short-grain white rice (like Arborio)

1 cinnamon stick

1 vanilla bean, split open (or 2 teaspoons pure vanilla extract)

1 cup raisins

½ cup dark rum

1. Place all the ingredients except for the raisins and rum into the pressure cooker. Stir well to ensure that the vanilla seeds are dispersed throughout. Lock the lid in place.

2. Pressure cook on HIGH for 12 minutes. While the rice pudding is cooking, combine the raisins and rum in a small saucepan and bring to a boil. Simmer for a couple of minutes and then remove from the heat and set aside.

3. Reduce the pressure with the QUICK-RELEASE method and carefully remove the lid.

4. Remove the vanilla bean and the cinnamon stick pieces from the pudding. Stir in the rum and raisins and serve with more half and half if desired.

 Thin leftover rice pudding with more milk or half and half. It will continue to get thicker as it sits in the fridge.

Coconut Rice Pudding with Pineapple

When you want to feel like you're in the tropics, this is the ticket! Instead of pineapple, try topping it with mango and strawberries for a change.

Serves	Prep	Cooking Time	Release Method
6 to 8	**Easiest**	**HIGH 12 Minutes**	**Quick**

1 (14 ounce) can coconut milk

2 cups half and half

1 cup whole milk

1 tablespoon butter

½ cup sugar

1½ cups short-grain white rice

1 cinnamon stick

⅛ teaspoon grated nutmeg

1 vanilla bean, split open OR
2 teaspoons pure vanilla extract

½ cup toasted shredded coconut

1 cup pineapple chunks

1. Place all the ingredients except the shredded coconut and pineapple into the pressure cooker. Stir well and lock the lid in place.

2. Pressure cook on HIGH for 12 minutes.

3. Reduce the pressure with the QUICK-RELEASE method and carefully remove the lid.

4. Stir the pudding and then let it sit for 5 minutes – it will thicken up as it sits. Garnish the pudding with the toasted coconut and pineapple chunks.

TIP Use a dry skillet to toast shredded coconut. Cook over medium heat, tossing regularly until the coconut is lightly browned. Remove immediately to a plate to avoid burning it.

Strawberry Rhubarb Compote with Balsamic Vinegar

While this is not the prettiest of compotes, it is super delicious! You can serve it over a variety of desserts from vanilla ice cream, to cheesecake to just a piece of cake, or use it as the base for a strawberry rhubarb crumble or pie.

Makes	Prep	Cooking Time	Release Method
1 Quart	**Easiest**	**HIGH 3 Minutes**	**Natural**

2 pounds rhubarb, chopped into 1-inch pieces

1 pound fresh strawberries, hulled and left whole

1 cup granulated sugar

1 cup apple cider

½ cup water

⅛ teaspoon salt

2 tablespoons balsamic vinegar

1. Combine all the ingredients except for the balsamic vinegar in the pressure cooker. Lock the lid in place.

2. Pressure cook on HIGH for 3 minutes.

3. Let the pressure drop NATURALLY and carefully remove the lid.

4. Transfer the fruit to a bowl with a slotted spoon and cool to room temperature. Add only as much liquid to the fruit to achieve the desired consistency. Stir in the balsamic vinegar and serve warm or cool over ice cream, cheesecake or pie.

TIP Rhubarb season starts early in April or May and goes through to the fall. Interestingly, the leaves of rhubarb are toxic, which is why you only see the stalks for sale in grocery stores.

Port Cherry Compote

What makes this compote so very easy to prepare is that it calls for frozen cherries. That means you don't have to pit fresh cherries AND you can enjoy it all year round.

Makes	Prep	Cooking Time	Release Method
1 Quart	**Easiest**	**HIGH 3 Minutes**	**Natural**

¾ cup port wine

½ cup brown sugar

2 tablespoons fresh lemon juice

2 teaspoons pure vanilla extract

½ cup water

2 pounds frozen cherries, pitted

1. Combine all ingredients in the pressure cooker and lock the lid in place.

2. Pressure cook on HIGH for 3 minutes.

3. Let the pressure drop NATURALLY and carefully remove the lid.

4. Transfer the fruit to a bowl and cool to room temperature. While the fruit cools, reduce the liquid by simmering using the BROWN setting for about 15 minutes. When the cherries are cool and ready to serve, add only as much liquid as will barely cover the fruit.

5. Serve over ice cream, cheesecake or pie.

TIP To get the most juice out of a lemon, roll it firmly on the counter for a few seconds or pop it in the microwave for 10 seconds before cutting in half and juicing.

Ginger Peach Compote

Makes	Prep	Cooking Time	Release Method
1 Quart	**Easiest**	**HIGH 3 Minutes**	**Natural**

2 pounds peeled, sliced frozen peaches

1 cup granulated sugar

1 cup white wine

5 thin slices fresh peeled gingerroot (about 1½-inches in diameter and ¼-inch thick)

½ cup water

1 tablespoon lemon juice

1. Combine all the ingredients in the pressure cooker and stir to dissolve the sugar. Lock the lid in place.

2. Pressure cook on HIGH for 3 minutes.

3. Let the pressure drop NATURALLY and carefully remove the lid.

4. Transfer the fruit to a bowl with a slotted spoon and remove the ginger slices. Add only as much liquid to the fruit to achieve the desired consistency. Serve warm or cool over ice cream, cheesecake or pie.

TIP The easiest way to peel ginger is with the back of your paring knife or with the edge of a teaspoon. Just rub the skin off. If the ginger is really young and the skin is thin, there's no need to peel it at all.

Blueberry Cinnamon Compote

Makes	Prep	Cooking Time	Release Method
2 Cups	**Easiest**	**HIGH 5 Minutes**	**Natural**

4 cups blueberries, fresh or frozen

⅔ cup granulated sugar

1 cup water

1 tablespoon lemon juice

1 cinnamon stick, broken in half

¼ teaspoon salt

pinch freshly ground black pepper

1. Combine all the ingredients in the pressure cooker and stir to dissolve the sugar. Lock the lid in place.

2. Pressure cook on HIGH for 5 minutes.

3. Let the pressure drop NATURALLY and carefully remove the lid.

4. Transfer the blueberries to a bowl with a slotted spoon and cool to room temperature. While the fruit cools, reduce the liquid in the cooker by simmering using the brown setting for about 15 minutes. Remove the cinnamon stick. Pour as much of the reduced liquid as you like over the blueberries. Serve over ice cream, cheesecake or pie.

TIP A small plastic container of blueberries is a little over one cup of berries. For this recipe, buy 4 small containers and you'll have a few left over for your morning cereal or yogurt!

Stewed Apples and Plums

Serves	Prep	Cooking Time	Release Method
6	**Easier**	**HIGH 3 Minutes**	**Quick**

1 cup red wine

1 cup apple cider

½ cup brown sugar

1 cinnamon stick

3 whole cloves

3 apples, peeled, cored and sliced

6 plums, pitted and cut into thin wedges (about 18 wedges per plum)

1. Combine the wine, cider, sugar, cinnamon and cloves in the pressure cooker and stir to dissolve the sugar. Add the apples and plums, mix well and lock the lid in place.

2. Pressure cook on HIGH for 3 minutes.

3. Reduce the pressure using the QUICK-RELEASE method and carefully remove the lid.

4. Remove the fruit from the cooker using a slotted spoon and set aside to cool. While the fruit cools, bring the liquid to a simmer using the BROWN setting and reduce by half. Pour the liquid over the fruit and serve warm or cool over ice cream, cheesecake or pie.

TIP There's not much difference between apple juice and apple cider – apple juice is filtered and pasteurized while apple cider is not. You can use either in this recipe.

Caramel Pot de Crème

Oh boy! This dessert is a head-slapper! It's smooth, creamy and delicious. If you like caramel, you'll LOVE this. Just remember that pot de crèmes really do need some time to cool before serving. They are best made several hours or even a day before you need them.

Serves	Prep	Cooking Time	Release Method
6	**Easy**	**HIGH 20 Minutes**	**Quick**

1½ cups sugar

¼ cup water

1 cup heavy cream

1 cup half and half

4 egg yolks

pinch salt

whipped cream (optional)

coarse sea salt (optional)

1. Combine the sugar and water in a saucepan. Over low heat, stir to dissolve the sugar. Increase the heat and bring the mixture to a boil. Stop stirring and instead swirl the pan every once in a while, as the sugar starts to brown and turn a deep amber color. Remove the pan from the heat and add the heavy cream and half and half. The mixture will bubble ferociously, but it will settle down and melt into a smooth liquid again when you return it to the heat. Stir over low heat until the caramel dissolves and then remove the pan from the heat.

2. In a separate bowl, beat the egg yolks until they are smooth and fall from the whisk like a ribbon. Whisk the warm caramel mixture into the egg yolks, adding the salt. (Should any of the egg form lumps, simply strain the mixture through a fine strainer.) Pour the mixture into 6 (4-ounce) ramekins and wrap each ramekin tightly in aluminum foil.

3. Pour enough water into the pressure cooker to cover the bottom by an inch. Place a rack in the bottom of the cooker and place the ramekins on the rack, stacking them on top of each other if necessary. Lock the lid in place.

4. Pressure cook on HIGH for 20 minutes.

5. Reduce the pressure with the QUICK-RELEASE method and carefully remove the lid.

6. Remove the ramekins from the cooker and unwrap them. They should still jiggle in the center. Cool at room temperature and then wrap with plastic wrap and refrigerate. Serve cold with a dollop of whipped cream, and a sprinkling of coarse sea salt if desired.

Dark Chocolate and Orange Pot de Crème

When I was a child, I would often get a Terry's ® dark chocolate orange for Christmas from Santa. Ever since, chocolate and orange has been a favorite combination of mine.

Serves	Prep	Cooking Time	Release Method
6	**Easy**	**HIGH 10 Minutes**	**Quick**

1 cup heavy cream

1 cup half and half

4 ounces bittersweet chocolate, chopped

2 ounces semi-sweet chocolate, chopped

1 tablespoon Grand Marnier®
or other orange liqueur

2 teaspoons finely grated orange zest

¼ cup sugar

4 egg yolks

pinch salt

whipped cream (optional)

candied orange peel (optional)

1. Combine the heavy cream and half and half in a saucepan. Heat gently over medium heat, stirring constantly until it just comes to a boil. Remove the pan from the heat and stir in the chocolates until the mixture is smooth. Stir in the Grand Marnier® and orange zest.

2. In a separate bowl, beat the sugar and egg yolks until they are smooth and fall from the whisk like a ribbon. Whisk the warm chocolate cream mixture into the egg yolks, adding the salt. (Should any of the egg form lumps, simply strain the mixture through a fine strainer.) Pour the mixture into 6 (4-ounce) ramekins and wrap each ramekin tightly in aluminum foil.

3. Pour enough water into the pressure cooker to cover the bottom by an inch. Place a rack in the bottom of the cooker and place the ramekins on the rack, stacking them on top of each other if necessary. Lock the lid in place.

4. Pressure cook on HIGH for 10 minutes.

5. Reduce the pressure with the QUICK-RELEASE method and carefully remove the lid. Remove the ramekins from the cooker and unwrap them. They should still jiggle in the center. Cool at room temperature and then wrap with plastic wrap and refrigerate. Serve cold with a dollop of whipped cream and some candied orange peel.

TIP Try not to over-cook these pot de crèmes. They should really jiggle in the center when finished – don't be tempted to continue cooking them. They will firm up in the refrigerator and be silky smooth in the center if cooked correctly.

Vanilla Cheesecake

Everyone seems stunned that a cheesecake can be made in a pressure cooker, but it's true. You'll still need time for the cheesecake to set up and cool after cooking, but the cooking time is greatly reduced with a pressure cooker. You will need a cake pan that will fit inside your cooker. I've found a 7-inch pan works in most cookers.

Serves	Prep	Cooking Time	Release Method
6	**Easy**	**HIGH 20 Minutes**	**Natural**

6 graham crackers, crushed

2 tablespoons butter, melted

1 pound cream cheese, room temperature

⅔ cup sugar

¾ teaspoon pure vanilla extract

2 eggs

1. Line the inside of a 7-inch cake pan with a large piece of greased aluminum foil (greased side facing up), pushing it into all the edges of the pan. Crush the graham crackers into crumbs either by hand or with a food processor, and combine with the melted butter. Press the crumb mixture into the base of the cake pan. Refrigerate while you prepare the cheesecake batter.

2. Using the paddle on your stand mixer with low speed, the regular beaters on a hand mixer on low speed, or a food processor, blend the cream cheese until it is completely smooth with no lumps. When all the lumps in the cream cheese have disappeared, add the sugar and vanilla extract. Blend just to incorporate the ingredients and then add the eggs one at a time. Continue to mix until the eggs have been mixed in, but do not over-beat.

3. Pour the batter into the cake pan with the graham cracker crust. Cover the pan tightly with more greased aluminum foil. Place a rack in the bottom of the pressure cooker. Make a sling with which to lower the cheesecake into the cooker by taking a long piece of aluminum foil, folding it in half lengthwise twice until it looks like it is about 26-inches by 3-inches. Lower the cheesecake into the cooker and onto the rack, and add enough water to cover the bottom by 1 inch. Lock the lid in place, tucking the ends of the sling into the cooker.

4. Pressure cook on HIGH for 20 minutes.

5. Let the pressure drop NATURALLY and let the cheesecake sit in the turned off pressure cooker for one hour. Carefully remove the lid and transfer the cheesecake from the cooker to the counter using the aluminum sling or rack. Let the cheesecake come to room temperature and then remove the foil from the top of the cake pan. Blot any liquid that might have condensed on the surface of the cake, wrap it in plastic wrap and refrigerate for at least 8 hours.

6. Bring the cake to room temperature before serving, and serve with any of the compotes in this book.

White Chocolate Raspberry Cheesecake

Serves	Prep	Cooking Time	Release Method
6	**Easy**	**HIGH 20 Minutes**	**Natural**

½ cup crushed vanilla wafers

¼ cup slivered almonds

2 tablespoons butter, melted

1 pound cream cheese, room temperature

⅔ cup sugar

¾ teaspoon pure vanilla extract

2 eggs

4 ounces white chocolate, chopped and melted

1 cup fresh raspberries, plus more for garnish

1. Line the inside of a 7-inch cake pan with a large piece of greased aluminum foil (greased side facing up), pushing it into all the edges of the pan. Crush the vanilla wafers and the almonds together in a food processor making a fine crumb. Mix the crumbs with the butter and press the crumb mixture into the base of the cake pan. Refrigerate while you prepare the cheesecake batter.

2. Using the paddle on your stand mixer with low speed, the regular beaters on a hand mixer on low speed, or a food processor, blend the cream cheese until it is completely smooth with no lumps. When all the lumps in the cream cheese have disappeared, add the sugar and vanilla extract. Blend just to incorporate the ingredients and then add the eggs one at a time. Continue to mix until the eggs have been mixed in, but do not over-beat. Gently stir in the melted white chocolate and then the raspberries.

3. Pour the batter into the cake pan with the vanilla wafer crust. Cover the pan tightly with more greased aluminum foil. Place a rack in the bottom of the pressure cooker. Make a sling with which to lower the cheesecake into the cooker by taking a long piece of aluminum foil, folding it in half lengthwise twice until it looks like it is about 26-inches by 3-inches. Lower the cheese-cake into the cooker and onto the rack, and add enough water to cover the bottom by 1 inch. Lock the lid in place, tucking the ends of the sling into the cooker.

4. Pressure cook on HIGH for 20 minutes.

5. Let the pressure drop NATURALLY and let the cheesecake sit in the turned off pressure cooker for one hour. Carefully remove the lid and transfer the cheesecake from the cooker to the counter using the aluminum sling or rack. Let the cheesecake come to room temperature and then remove the foil from the top of the cake pan. Blot any liquid that might have condensed on the surface of the cake, wrap it in plastic wrap and refrigerate for at least 8 hours.

6. Bring the cake to room temperature before serving, and serve with more fresh raspberries.

Chocolate Chunk Cheesecake

Depending on the chocolate chips or chunks that you use, the chocolate may sink to the bottom of the cheesecake while it cooks. Not to worry, you'll end up with a layered cheesecake and no-one I've known has every complained about that!

Serves	Prep	Cooking Time	Release Method
6	**Easy**	**HIGH 20 Minutes**	**Natural**

½ cup crushed Oreo® cookies

1 pound cream cheese, room temperature

⅔ cup sugar

¾ teaspoon pure vanilla extract

2 eggs

4 ounces chocolate chunks

1. Line the inside of a 7-inch cake pan with a large piece of greased aluminum foil (greased side facing up), pushing it into all the edges of the pan. Crush the Oreo® cookies, combining the filling and the cookie crumbs. Press the crumb mixture into the base of the cake pan. Refrigerate while you prepare the cheesecake batter.

2. Using the paddle on your stand mixer with low speed, the regular beaters on a hand mixer on low speed, or a food processor, blend the cream cheese until it is completely smooth with no lumps. When all the lumps in the cream cheese have disappeared, add the sugar and vanilla extract. Blend just to incorporate the ingredients and then add the eggs one at a time. Continue to mix until the eggs have been mixed in, but do not over-beat. Gently stir in the chocolate chunks.

3. Pour the batter into the cake pan with the Oreo® cookie crust. Cover the pan tightly with more greased aluminum foil. Place a rack in the bottom of the pressure cooker. Make a sling with which to lower the cheesecake into the cooker by taking a long piece of aluminum foil, folding it in half lengthwise twice until it looks like it is about 26-inches by 3-inches. Lower the cheese-cake into the cooker and onto the rack, and add enough water to cover the bottom by 1 inch. Lock the lid in place, tucking the ends of the sling into the cooker.

4. Pressure cook on HIGH for 20 minutes.

5. Let the pressure drop NATURALLY and let the cheesecake sit in the turned off pressure cooker for one hour. Carefully remove the lid and transfer the cheesecake from the cooker to the counter using the aluminum sling or rack. Let the cheesecake come to room temperature and then remove the foil from the top of the cake pan. Blot any liquid that might have condensed on the surface of the cake, wrap it in plastic wrap and refrigerate for at least 8 hours.

6. Bring the cake to room temperature before serving, and serve with whipped cream if desired.

Bread and Butter Pudding

Bread and Butter Pudding is a beautiful thing! The key is to use good-sized pieces of bread, rather than thin slices. You can even use Challah or croissants, or decadent brioche bread instead of white bread. Just make sure whatever bread you use is stale or oven-dried. That way it will absorb more of the delicious custard.

Serves	Prep	Cooking Time	Release Method
8	**Easy**	**HIGH 25 Minutes**	**Natural**

1 cup milk

1 cup heavy cream
(plus more for serving if desired)

¾ cup granulated or brown sugar

1 vanilla bean, split open OR
2 teaspoons pure vanilla extract

1 teaspoon ground cinnamon

pinch ground nutmeg

4 eggs

12 slices stale Texas toast (or thick slices of any dense white bread)

4 ounces butter, softened

1 cup raisins

1. Grease a 2-quart ceramic soufflé dish or metal baking pan with butter.

2. Combine the milk, heavy cream, sugar, vanilla bean, cinnamon and nutmeg in a saucepan and bring to a simmer, stirring to dissolve the sugar. Lightly beat the eggs in a bowl. Temper the eggs into the milk mixture by adding a little milk to the eggs, beating, and then adding the eggs back into the milk mixture.

3. Butter each slice of bread and then cut the slices into quartered triangles. Place one layer of overlapping triangles into the soufflé dish. Scatter raisins on top and then pour in some of the milk mixture. Repeat these layers, ending with a layer of bread and the remaining milk mixture. Press down on the pudding with your hands to help the bread absorb the custard, and let the pudding sit until most of the liquid has been absorbed. Wrap the soufflé dish tightly with greased aluminum foil.

4. Place a trivet or steamer rack in the pressure cooker and add 2 cups of water. Lower the soufflé dish into the cooker using a sling made of aluminum foil (fold a piece of aluminum foil into a strip about 3-inches wide by 26-inches long). Lock the lid in place.

5. Pressure cook on HIGH for 25 minutes.

6. Let the pressure drop NATURALLY and carefully remove the lid.

7. Remove the pudding from the cooker and let it cool. This can be served warm or cold with a little heavy cream poured over top.

TIP

If the bread you have is not stale, you can leave it out on a baking sheet overnight, or pop it into a 350° F oven for 15 minutes or until it feels dry. Dry, or stale bread is more absorbent and soaks up more of the custard in a bread pudding.

Annie's Chocolate Hazelnut Banana Bread and Butter Pudding

Annie gets credit for this dessert for coming up with the idea of adding bananas. The flavor combination of chocolate, hazelnuts and banana can't be beat! Annie has great taste!

Serves	Prep	Cooking Time	Release Method
8	**Easy**	**HIGH 25 Minutes**	**Natural**

1 cup milk

1 cup heavy cream (plus more for serving if desired)

¾ cup granulated or brown sugar

1 vanilla bean, split open OR 2 teaspoons pure vanilla extract

1 teaspoon ground cinnamon

pinch ground nutmeg

4 eggs

12 slices stale Texas toast or Challah (or thick slices of any dense white bread)

4 ounces butter, softened

1 (13-ounce) jar Nutella® chocolate hazelnut spread

½ cup hazelnuts, toasted and chopped

2 bananas, peeled and sliced

1. Grease a 2-quart ceramic soufflé dish or metal baking pan with butter.

2. Combine the milk, heavy cream, sugar, vanilla bean, cinnamon and nutmeg in a saucepan and bring to a simmer, stirring to dissolve the sugar. Lightly beat the eggs in a bowl. Temper the eggs into the milk mixture by adding a little milk to the eggs, beating, and then adding the eggs back into the milk mixture.

3. Butter each slice of bread and then spread Nutella® on top. Cut the slices into quartered triangles. Place one layer of overlapping triangles into the soufflé dish. Scatter hazelnuts and banana slices on top and then pour in some of the milk mixture. Repeat these layers, ending with a layer of bread and the remaining milk mixture. Press down on the pudding with your hands to help the bread absorb the custard, and let the pudding sit until most of the liquid has been absorbed. Wrap the soufflé dish tightly with greased aluminum foil.

4. Place a trivet or steamer rack in the pressure cooker and add 2 cups of water. Lower the soufflé dish into the cooker using a sling made of aluminum foil (fold a piece of aluminum foil into a strip about 3-inches wide by 26-inches long). Lock the lid in place.

5. Pressure cook on HIGH for 25 minutes.

6. Let the pressure drop NATURALLY and carefully remove the lid.

7. Remove the pudding from the cooker and let it cool. This can be served warm or cold with a little heavy cream poured over top.

Marmalade Bread and Butter Pudding

This is a very pretty bread and butter pudding because of the orange peel in the marmalade. While most bread and butter puddings are served for dessert, this one could be served for breakfast too.

Serves	Prep	Cooking Time	Release Method
8	**Easy**	**HIGH 25 Minutes**	**Natural**

1 cup milk

1 cup heavy cream (plus more for serving if desired)

¾ cup granulated or brown sugar

1 vanilla bean, split open OR
2 teaspoons pure vanilla extract

1 teaspoon ground cinnamon

pinch ground nutmeg

4 eggs

12 slices stale Texas toast or Challah (or thick slices of any dense white bread)

4 ounces butter, softened

1 (13 ounce) jar orange marmalade

1 cup raisins

1. Grease a 2-quart ceramic soufflé dish or metal baking pan with butter.

2. Combine the milk, heavy cream, sugar, vanilla bean, cinnamon and nutmeg in a saucepan and bring to a simmer, stirring to dissolve the sugar. Lightly beat the eggs in a bowl. Temper the eggs into the milk mixture by adding a little milk to the eggs, beating, and then adding the eggs back into the milk mixture.

3. Butter each slice of bread and then generously spread marmalade on top. Cut the slices into quartered triangles. Place one layer of overlapping triangles into the soufflé dish. Scatter raisins on top and then pour in some of the milk mixture. Repeat these layers, ending with a layer of bread and the remaining milk mixture. Press down on the pudding with your hands to help the bread absorb the custard, and let the pudding sit until most of the liquid has been absorbed. Wrap the soufflé dish tightly with greased aluminum foil.

4. Place a trivet or steamer rack in the pressure cooker and add 2 cups of water. Lower the soufflé dish into the cooker using a sling made of aluminum foil (fold a piece of aluminum foil into a strip about 3-inches wide by 26-inches long). Lock the lid in place.

5. Pressure cook on HIGH for 25 minutes.

6. Let the pressure drop NATURALLY and carefully remove the lid.

7. Remove the pudding from the cooker and let it cool. This can be served warm or cold with a little heavy cream poured over top.

Toffee Apple Bread Pudding

Serves	Prep	Cooking Time	Release Method
8	**Easy**	**HIGH 25 Minutes**	**Natural**

1 cup milk

1 cup heavy cream (plus more for serving if desired)

¾ cup granulated or brown sugar

1 vanilla bean, split open OR
2 teaspoons pure vanilla extract

1 teaspoon ground cinnamon

pinch ground nutmeg

4 eggs

1 pound stale or toasted Challah bread, cubed (about 6 cups)

3 Granny Smith apples, peeled and cut into chunks

8 ounces toffee chips

1. Grease a 2-quart ceramic soufflé dish or metal baking pan with butter.

2. Combine the milk, heavy cream, sugar, vanilla bean, cinnamon and nutmeg in a saucepan and bring to a simmer, stirring to dissolve the sugar. Lightly beat the eggs in a bowl. Temper the eggs into the milk mixture by adding a little milk to the eggs, beating, and then adding the eggs back into the milk mixture.

3. Toss the challah with the apple and toffee chips in a large bowl and then transfer to the buttered soufflé dish. Pour the egg custard over the top. Press down on the pudding with your hands to help the bread absorb the custard, and let the pudding sit until most of the liquid has been absorbed. Wrap the soufflé dish tightly with greased aluminum foil.

4. Place a trivet or steamer rack in the pressure cooker and add 2 cups of water. Lower the soufflé dish into the cooker using a sling made of aluminum foil (fold a piece of aluminum foil into a strip about 3-inches wide by 26-inches long). Lock the lid in place.

5. Pressure cook on HIGH for 25 minutes.

6. Let the pressure drop NATURALLY and carefully remove the lid.

7. Remove the pudding from the cooker and let it cool. This can be served warm with some vanilla ice cream.

Index

Index

Index

Index

Tip Index

Notes

Notes

Notes

Notes

Notes

Notes